THE ANCIENT EGYPTIAN BOOK OF TWO WAYS

THE ANCIENT EGYPTIAN BOOK OF TWO WAYS

By LEONARD H. LESKO

UNIVERSITY OF CALIFORNIA PRESS
BERKELEY · LOS ANGELES · LONDON

UNIVERSITY OF CALIFORNIA PUBLICATIONS
NEAR EASTERN STUDIES
Volume 17

UNIVERSITY OF CALIFORNIA PRESS
BERKELEY AND LOS ANGELES
CALIFORNIA

UNIVERSITY OF CALIFORNIA PRESS, LTD.
LONDON, ENGLAND

ISBN: 0-520-03514-3
LIBRARY OF CONGRESS CATALOG CARD NO. 72-83096

© 1972 BY THE REGENTS OF THE UNIVERSITY OF CALIFORNIA
CALIFORNIA LIBRARY REPRINT SERIES EDITION, 1977

1 2 3 4 5 6 7 8 9 0

CONTENTS

PREFACE vii

ABBREVIATIONS viii

LIST OF SYMBOLS xi

PLATE: THE TWO DIFFERENT PLANS OF THE
        BOOK OF TWO WAYS xii

INTRODUCTION 1

DESCRIPTION, TRANSLATION AND NOTES:

    SECTION   I 11

    SECTION   II 25

    SECTION   III 40

    SECTION   IV 61

    SECTION   V 77

    SECTION   VI 93

    SECTION   VII 102

    SECTION VIII 109

    SECTION   IX 120

CONCLUSION 134

INDEX OF CT SPELLS 140

BOOK OF THE DEAD PARALLELS 142

INDEX OF SELECTED VOCABULARY 143

PREFACE

A description of the Book of Two Ways with translations of half of its texts was included in my doctoral dissertation, The Composition of the Book of Two Ways, which was submitted to the Department of Near Eastern Languages and Civilizations of the University of Chicago in March, 1969.

I wish to express my thanks to the readers of the original dissertation, Professors Edward F. Wente, George R. Hughes, and Klaus Baer for many valuable suggestions concerned with its translation, form, and style. I am particularly indebted to Professor John A. Wilson who directed the dissertation and continued to coordinate the efforts of my committee even after his retirement.

In the past three years I have further revised almost all the translations so that I alone must accept responsibility for them. The description is presented here in a rather straightforward manner based to a large extent on the conclusions reached in my article entitled "Some Observations on the Composition of the Book of Two Ways," in the Journal of the American Oriental Society 91 (1971).

I thank the University of California and particularly the Chairmen of the Department of Near Eastern Studies at Berkeley for their interest in and support of this project. I thank the University of California Press for including this monograph in its Near Eastern Studies Series. I am very grateful to Mrs. Henry Lynn, Jr. for typing the manuscript in its final form and to Mrs. Adrienne Morgan for her drawing of the sample plans.

I would like to dedicate this book to my wife, Barbara, for her patience and encouragement throughout the past six years.

Berkeley   Leonard H. Lesko

ABBREVIATIONS

AEB	Annual Egyptological Bibliography, Leiden, 1948--.
Amduat	Hornung, Erik. Das Amduat: Die Schrift des verborgenen Raumes. (Ägyptologische Abhandlungen, Band 7, 13.) 3 parts. Wiesbaden: Harrassowitz, 1963-67.
ASAE	Egypt, Service des Antiquités, Annales, Le Caire, 1900--.
B	el Barsha, (As designation of provenience of coffins, e.g., B1C, the first el Barsha coffin in the Cairo museum to receive a designation by the editors of the Coffin Texts.) This is distinct from version B.
BD	Book of the Dead (followed by the number of the chapter). Budge, E. A. W. The Book of the Dead: an English Translation, 2nd ed., London, 1910. Allen, Thomas George. The Egyptian Book of the Dead. Documents in the Oriental Institute Museum. (Oriental Institute Publication, vol. 82) Chicago, 1960. Barguet, Paul. Le Livre des Morts des Anciens Égyptiens. (Litteratures Anciennes du Proche-Orient) Paris, 1967.
Be	Berlin, Staatliche Museen.
BibO	Bibliotheca Orientalis, Leyden, 1944--.
BIFAO	Cairo, Institut français d'archéologie orientale, Bulletin, Le Caire, 1901--.
Bo	Boston, Museum of Fine Arts.
Book of Gates	Maystre, Charles and Alexandre Piankoff. Le Livre des Portes. Vol. I (3 fascicles). (Memoires de l'Institut Français du Caire, Tome 74.) Le Caire, 1939, 1944, 1946. Piankoff, Alexandre. Le Livre des Portes. Vol. II (2 fascicles) and vol. III. (Memoires, T. 75 and 90) Le Caire, 1961, 1962.
Borghouts, Magical Texts	Borghouts, J. F. The Magical Texts of Papyrus Leiden I 348 (Oudheidkundige Mededelingen, 51) Leiden, 1970.
C	Cairo, Musée des antiquités, (as distinct from version C).

CDME	Faulkner, Raymond O. *A Concise Dictionary of Middle Egyptian.* Oxford, 1962.
CT	Coffin Texts, (followed by the number of the spell).
ECT	Buck, Adriaan de. *The Egyptian Coffin Texts.* Vols. I-VII (Oriental Institute Publications, vols. 34, 49, 64, 67, 73, 81, 87) Chicago: 1935-1961.
Edel, Alt. Gram.	Edel, Elmar. *Altägyptische Grammatik.* Vols. I and II. (Analecta Orientalia, vols. 34, 39) Rome, 1955-1964.
Gard.	Gardiner, Sir Alan H. *Egyptian Grammar.* 3rd ed., Oxford, 1957.
Hekanakhte	James, T. G. H. *The Hekanakhte Papers and Other Early Middle Kingdom Documents.* (Metropolitan Museum of Art, Publications, 19.) New York, 1962.
JAOS	*Journal of the American Oriental Society.* New Haven, 1843--.
JARCE	*Journal of the American Research Center in Egypt.* Boston, 1962--.
JEA	*Journal of Egyptian Archaeology.* London, 1914--.
JEOL	*Jaarbericht van het Vooraziatisch-Egyptisch Genootshap "Ex Oriente Lux."* Leiden, 1933--.
JNES	*Journal of Near Eastern Studies.* Chicago, 1942--.
Kees, Totenglauben	Kees, Hermann. *Totenglauben und Jenseitsvorstellungen der alten Ägypter.* 2nd ed., Berlin, 1956.
L	London, British Museum.
LEM	Caminos, Ricardo A. *Late-Egyptian Miscellanies.* (Brown Egyptological Studies, 1.) London, 1954.
MDAIK	*Mitteilungen des Deutschen Archäologischen Instituts,* Abteilung, Kairo.
MIFAO	Mémoires publiés par les membres de l'Institut Français d'Archéologie Orientale du Caire. Cairo, 1902--.
OIP	Chicago, *Oriental Institute Publications.*
OLZ	*Orientalistische Literaturzeitung.* Berlin and Leipzig, 1898--.

NAWG	Nachrichten der Akademie der Wissenschaften in Göttingen.
P	Paris, Louvre.
Polotsky, "Tenses"	Polotsky, Hans Jakob, "Egyptian Tenses," *Proceedings of the Israel Academy of Sciences and Humanities*. Vol. II, No. 5, 1965.
PT	Pyramid Texts, (followed by the number of the Utterance). Sethe, Kurt. *Altägyptischen Pyramidentexte*. 4 Bde. Leipzig, 1908-1922. Sethe, Kurt. *Übersetzung und Kommentar zu den altägyptischen Pyramidentexten*. 6 bde. Glückstadt, (no date)-1962. Speleers, Louis. *Traduction, Index et Vocabulaire des Textes des Pyramides Égyptiennes*. Bruxelles, 1946. Mercer, Samuel A. B. *The Pyramid Texts; in Translation and Commentary*. New York, 1952. Faulkner, Raymond O. *The Ancient Egyptian Pyramid Texts*. Oxford, 1969.
Rd'É	*Revue d'égyptologie*, Le Caire, 1933--.
Roccati, Papiro Ieratico	Roccati, Alessandro. *Papiro Ieratico n.54003: Estratti magici e rituali del Primo Medio Regno* (Catalogo del Museo Egizio di Torino, Serie Prima, vol. 2) Torino, 1970.
TPPI	Clère, J. J. et J. Vandier. *Textes de la Première Période Intermédiaire et de la XIème Dynastie*. Bruxelles, 1948.
Urk.	Sethe, Kurt. *Urkunden der 18. Dynastie*. Leipzig, 1961.
WAD	Von Deines, Hildegard und Hermann Grapow. *Wörterbuch der ägyptischen Drogennamen*. Berlin, 1959.
Wb.	Erman, Adolf und Hermann Grapow. *Wörterbuch der aegyptischen Sprache*. 7 vols., Leipzig, 1926-63.
WMT	Von Deines, Hildegard und Wolfhart Westendorf. *Wörterbuch der medizinischen Texte*. 2 vols., Berlin, 1961-62.
Zandee, *Death*.	Zandee, Jan. *Death as an Enemy*. Leiden, 1960.
ZÄS	*Zeitschrift für ägyptische Sprache und Altertumskunde*. Leipzig, 1863-1943, Berlin, 1954--.

SYMBOLS

[ ] . . . . . lost
⌈ ⌉ . . . . . uncertain (reading or meaning)
{ } . . . . . superfluous
( ) . . . . . supplied or comment
⟨ ⟩ . . . . . emended by editor
... . omitted by editor
⟨ . . . . . developed out of
⟩ . . . . . developed into

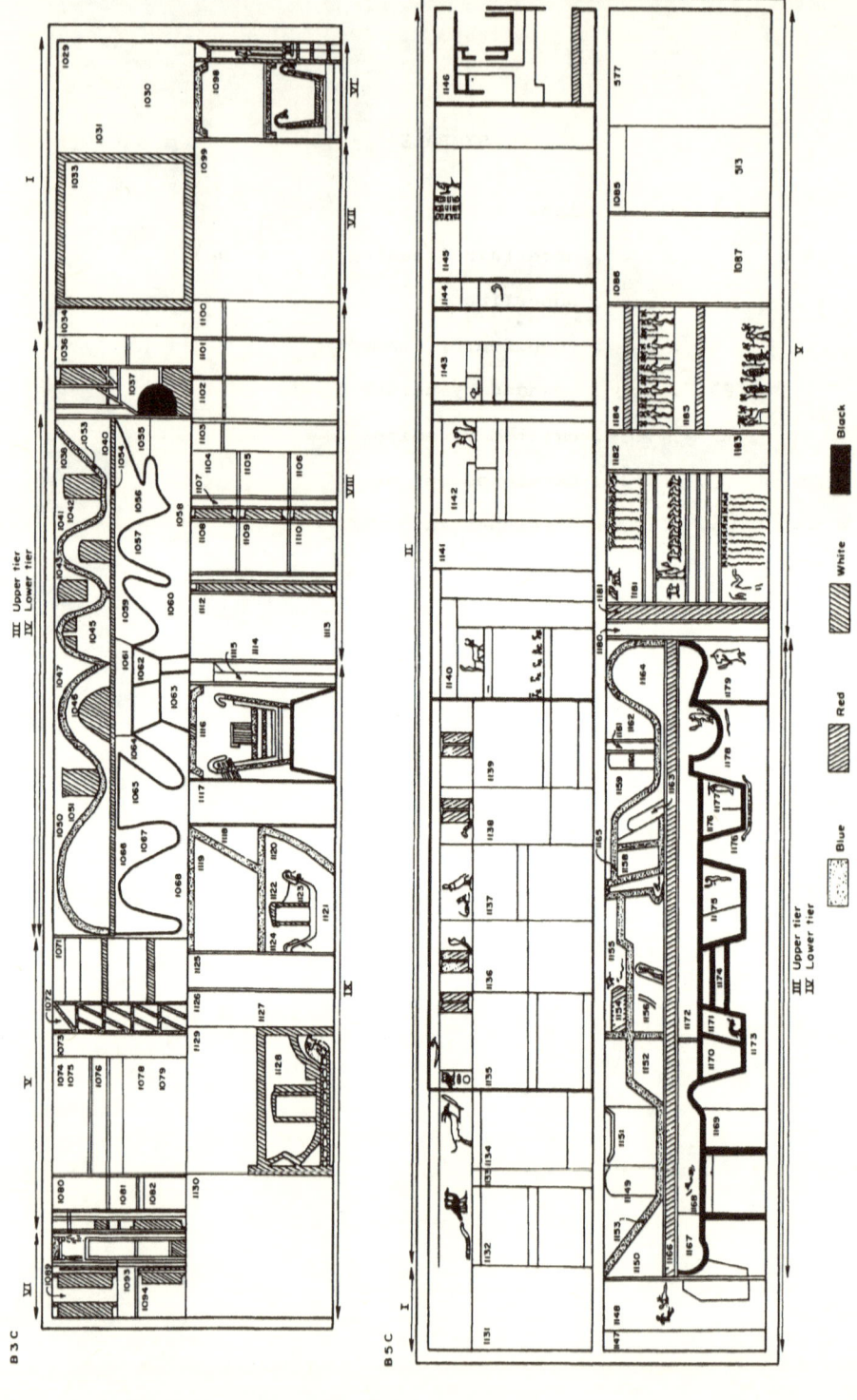

INTRODUCTION

A considerable amount of religious literature has survived from ancient Egypt. The Egyptians had an elaborate mythology and an extensive calendar of feasts. Their temple libraries undoubtedly contained a large number of books to describe the myths, indicate the rituals to be observed at the feasts, and also to provide the hymns and prayers that would have been necessary for any eventuality. Although some of this has survived intact, most of what we have comes from the selection of texts that individuals took to the grave with them. Much of this is concerned with providing for a life after death, and the selections included material from religious books that they hoped would be of use to a person in the next life or would even put off death temporarily if read by a living person. In addition to the myths, rituals, prayers, and hymns, these collections also contain a large number of purely magical spells and fanciful descriptions.

Apparently the collections from which the copyist or the deceased could choose became more or less standardized in different periods and in different places. The three largest collections of texts correspond roughly to the three main divisions of Egyptian history. In the Old Kingdom (2664-2155 B.C.), kings, beginning with Unis of the Fifth Dynasty, had texts carved on the walls of the inner chambers of their pyramids at Sakkara. The kings of the Sixth Dynasty used many of the same texts but deleted some parts and added others from a collection of probably more than the 759 "Utterances" that survive. Although these Pyramid Texts were generally intended for the king alone, they were copied also in queens' burial chambers, and later, in the Middle Kingdom, nobles, men and women, used some of them on their tombs and coffins, and nobles of the Twenty-fifth and Twenty-sixth Dynasties returned to this collection for the selection of texts to be included on their tombs and sarcophagi.

The second collection comes principally from the coffins of nobles of the First Intermediate Period and the early Middle

Kingdom (2154-1845 B.C.). While the texts were usually written with brush and ink on the inside surfaces (sides, top, and bottom) of the wooden coffins of wealthy noblemen from Middle and Upper Egypt, they are also found on Canopic boxes, cartonnage masks, limestone coffins, tomb walls, a statue, and a stela. The 1,185 "Spells" of the Coffin Texts also include some texts from Old Kingdom papyri and exclude texts from Middle Kingdon coffins that have been edited as Pyramid Texts, so that the only way to categorize Coffin Texts now is as non-royal funerary literature antecedent to the Book of the Dead.

Some portion of the 190 "Chapters" of the Book of the Dead were copied on papyri with vignettes or illustrations, and these books were available to anyone who could afford them from the New Kingdom (1554-1075 B.C.) through the Ptolemaic Period. In the Coffin Texts, stress was occasionally put on acceptable standards of morality and the Book of the Dead perhaps shows some progress in its addition of a negative confession and a judgement scene, but because of the more frequent addition of explanatory glosses to the statements of moral uprightness from Coffin Texts, these same statements often become merely "avowals of ritualistic action" in the Book of the Dead.[1]

In addition to these three major groups of texts, Egyptian mortuary literature also includes several collections of illustrated texts mainly from New Kingdom royal tombs at Thebes, and these comprise a subgroup that is known as "guides to the beyond."[2] These often include maps of the underworld with pictures and names of the gatekeepers and demons encountered on the way to a goal, and also the spells to be recited in order to pass them and reach the goal. Such collections as the Book of Gates, the Book of Caves, and Amduat (the book of that which is in the netherworld) have been published now, and though difficult, inconsistent, and often enigmatic, should contribute to our knowledge of ancient Egyptian religion. The earliest known example of this type of literature is also part and parcel of the Middle Kingdom non-royal Coffin Texts, the so-called Book of Two Ways.

Of all ancient Egyptian mortuary literature, Coffin Texts are by far the largest collection but also the least known and least studied. The 1,185 spells, not counting those taken from Pyramid Texts, were edited and published in transcription in

Introduction 3

seven volumes by the late Adriaan de Buck between 1935 and 1961.[3] De Buck died before he could complete the work with an introduction, translations, commentary, and glossary as Breasted had originally planned.[4] A translation of the first two volumes has appeared[5] and some other parts of the material have been translated and used in various studies, but really very little has been done.

The Book of Two Ways received its name from Schack-Schackenburg who in 1903 published photos and facsimile copies of the texts on the bottom of a coffin in Berlin.[6] A few years later Lacau published similar texts from the coffins in the Cairo Museum,[7] and the de Buck edition includes the texts from these and other coffins that have the "book" reasonably well preserved.[8]

Though Coffin Texts are known from a number of sites in ancient Egypt, all eighteen published and four unpublished coffins that have the Book of Two Ways are apparently from el Barsha, a necropolis of Hermopolis, capital of the Hare nome in Middle Egypt.

Several descriptions of the Book of Two Ways with varying interpretations have been presented over the years,[9] but a translation of all of the spells involved in the work has not yet appeared. The texts are difficult, but with very little enigmatic writing; more often they were abbreviated or somewhat garbled from copying. The problem of interpretation comes from the juxtaposition of various traditions, the syncretism characteristic of Egyptian religion, and our own lack of knowledge about the background of the Egyptians' myths and rituals. The translations that follow are to be regarded as a pioneering attempt and in no way definitive. The translations are eclectic based on what I consider to be the best text. The translations are also uneven with some passages quite intelligible and others quite impossible. But this is as it must be since the work was composed from earlier material which often degenerated through the errors of copyists. The notes that follow the translation of each spell present the texts of the important variants, less likely alternative translations, and justification for my translations when justification is needed. In some manuscripts the owner of the coffin is named or referred to in the third person whenever he occurs in the text, but, since there is evidence that all of these mss. were copied from texts in the first person, I have regularly used first person pronouns.

The nine sections of the Book of Two Ways are based partly on the emphasis within the texts on one or another god or goal. The separate sections will be seen to be different traditions about the afterlife, each apparently complete in itself. Re and Osiris each have several of these sections in which they are stressed individually, and the goal of the deceased varies accordingly. Thoth as the local god of Hermopolis also figures importantly in one section. For two versions of the book, the various traditions which comprise the whole can be shown to have had their separate goals resumed at the end and these goals are related to one another here, perhaps with social implications.[10]

An attempt will be made to compare the texts of the coffins within each version, but this is often difficult because of incomplete copying from an original, the present state of preservation of the mss. and the close connections that are found even among the coffins with different versions.

One point in our favor is the fact that we have vignettes accompanying the texts, and so can identify the names and epithets applied to the gods, demons, localities, and, in one case at least, to the deceased.

Usually the Book of Two Ways was copied on the inside bottoms of the nobles' coffins, probably so that the deceased would have this guide at their feet when waking in the underworld.[11] The book received its name because of the two zigzag paths that form a kind of map for the use of the deceased. This map section generally takes up about one-third of the whole book, but on one coffin it is repeated and on other coffins the plan is omitted though the texts that usually accompany it occur in varying stages of completeness. For the other two-thirds of the book, the texts and plans follow one of two different patterns. When all of these texts are combined in their proper order taking into account what the two different groups have in common, we lose a little of the original consecutiveness of each but gain a great deal in being able to compare them. The Book of Two Ways is divided into nine sections which are generally easy to distinguish. The texts actually occur in three different versions or variants which I have labeled A, B, and C.

Introduction

The A and B versions of the texts are longer and are found in a plan of the book that includes sections I, III, IV, V, VI, VII, VIII, and IX. Version C occurs on a shorter plan that includes sections I, II, III, IV, and V. Section I includes the two very different introductions to the two groups, and therefore the groups are similar to one another only in sections III, IV, and V.

Before proceeding to the texts themselves a brief resumé of the religious traditions reflected in them might be useful. In the Pyramid Texts the deceased king ascends to the sky in a variety of ways and by different means. He joins the sun god, Re, on the bark in which Re sails through the sky during the day and through the underworld at night. These texts include a large number of spells to give the deceased king power to overcome or pass the demons, often snakes, who try to hinder the progress of the sun bark. The goal of the deceased king then is to guide the bark of the sun god and being a god himself, the "son of Re" as king on earth, at death with his own son as the "son of Re," he can identify himself with Re and he does.

An apparently earlier myth of divine kingship involves the struggle of the two brothers, Osiris and Seth, for the throne. Osiris who was murdered by Seth was avenged by his son Horus so that Osiris became the king of the dead and his son became Horus the king of Egypt. This myth is also reflected in numerous references in the Pyramid Texts and perhaps quite significantly in the king's being addressed as Horus in the first texts in the passage leading into the antechamber of his burial place but being addressed as Osiris after he has ascended to the sky in the texts of the inner chambers.

While the myth of Horus and Osiris goes through the Pyramid Texts as an undercurrent, the principal stress in the Pyramid Texts is on the Solar myth and without overemphasizing a "Re revolution" we can still see the influence of the Heliopolitan priesthood of Re in the sudden appearance of sun-temples and Pyramid Texts in the Fifth Dynasty.

Coffin Texts have been characterized by their "democratization of the hereafter" and this is generally taken as indicating that First Intermediate Period and Middle Kingdom noblemen have taken over texts that would only have been available to the king in earlier times. Even though we know now that some <u>Pyramid Texts</u> were non-royal and that some <u>Coffin Texts</u> are from the Old Kingdom, this is still a good characterization as we shall see. <u>Coffin Texts</u> include a large number of myths and descriptions of the afterlife and although the deceased can be identified with both Re and Osiris, he is not always that lucky. Some texts obviously intended for the deceased commoner to be a servant for the other gods in the afterlife or at least to share in some lesser capacity in the afterlife of the king as one or the other of the major gods probably depending to some extent on which of these gods had more personal appeal or where the person came from. If we can explain how these lesser goals can occur together with the highest goals on the coffins of nobles then we might be able to explain how, when and why the hereafter became democratized.

The <u>Book of Two Ways</u> includes a number of different gods and goals so this is a good place to begin looking for the answers to these questions about the <u>Coffin Texts</u>. In addition to Re and Osiris the <u>Book of Two Ways</u> also involves Thoth the god of the moon who is accompanied in the sky at night by the deceased as stars. To some extent he is as important as the other gods providing as he does a goal for the deceased, but since all the coffins having these texts are from his city this is not surprising. What is more unusual is to have this same Thoth in other texts within the <u>Book of Two Ways</u> as a mere attendant of Osiris.

The last major deity in these texts is Horus, but not only the Horus who avenges his father Osiris in the famous myth. This is Horus, the eldest son of Re, who with wings outstretched represents the whole sky with his eyes as the sun and moon, the latter having been injured in the conflict with Seth. Seth who should be a villain, then, can also turn up unexpectedly as one of the guides on the bark of Re at the end of the book where the principal villain is the serpent Apopis who tries to devour the solar bark.

For goals of the deceased in the <u>Book of Two Ways</u> there is not only the famous "Field of Offerings" or "Elysian Fields," but also the mansion or palace of Osiris,[12] the mansion of the moon, and the solar bark. Of the demons who guard the flaming red gates many are the same as those known from the two chapters (144 and 147) of the <u>Book of the Dead</u> devoted to the subject of gatekeepers. The Book of the Dead has seven in each chapter and they are thought to have come from separate traditions. The Book of Two Ways has two more groups of keepers and in one group there are seven gates.

Spells presumably are concerned with helping the deceased reach the goals, but it should be noted that there are almost no moral criteria connected with reaching the goals in the Book of Two Ways. If a person could afford to buy the guide, having it was supposed to be enough to guarantee his future life. This could still make some sense if the deceased would have been able to read the book or memorize its contents, but, since the copies were so incomplete and replete with errors, it is questionable whether many of the owners would have or could have read the texts. The scribes who copied the texts were not too concerned with the deceased reaching his goal, but the scribe or scribes who composed the book (really the two books) certainly had something in mind and this is what we are looking for. We shall see that the second, longer version of the book is concerned precisely with the relationship of the various goals. What we learn about the origin and composition of this work from a study of the form and content of its versions and sections is probably unique in Egyptian religious literature.

Notes to Introduction

[1] John A. Wilson, *The Burden of Egypt* (Chicago: The University of Chicago Press, 1951), p. 118.

[2] Hermann Kees, *Totenglauben und Jenseitsvorstellungen der Alten Ägypter* (2nd ed.; Berlin [originally Leipzig, 1926], 1956) pp. 287-302.

[3] Adriaan de Buck, *The Egyptian Coffin Texts* (OIP, vols. 34, 49, 64, 67, 73, 81, 87; Chicago: University of Chicago Press, 1935-1961), Vols. I-VII.

[4] James H. Breasted, *The Oriental Institute* (Chicago: The University of Chicago Press, 1933), pp. 167-168.

[5] Louis Speelers, *Textes des cercueils du Moyen Empire égyptien* (Bruxelles, 1947).

[6] Hans Schack-Schackenburg, *Das Buch von den Zwei Wegen des seligen Toten* (Leipzig, 1903).

[7] Pierre Lacau, *Sarcophages antérieurs au Nouvel Empire*, Vols. I-II (Catalogue général des Antiquités égyptiennes du Musée du Caire, 1904-1906).

[8] Adriaan de Buck, *op. cit.*, Vol. VII.

[9] Hermann Grapow, "Zweiwegebuch und Totenbuch," *ZÄS*, 46 (1909) 77-81; Hermann Kees, *Totenglauben*; Jacques Vandier, *La Religion Égyptienne* ("Mana"; Paris, 1949), pp. 91-93; Hermann Grapow, "Jenseitsführer," in B. Spuler, *Handbuch der Orientalistik* (Leiden, 1952) I, part 2; Wilhelm Bonacker, "The Egyptian 'Book of the Two Ways'," *Imago Mundi* 7 (1951) 5-17; Hans Bonnet, *Reallexikon der Ägyptischen Religionsgeschichte* (Berlin, 1952) pp. 882-883; Jan Zandee, "De Reis van de Dode," *JEOL* No. 15 (1957-58) 65-71; Jozef M. A. Janssen, "De Bodem van Sarcofaag Cairo 28087," *JEOL* No. 15 (1957-58) 71-73; Jan Zandee, rev. of *ECT* VII in *AEB* (1961) 31-44; Philippe Derchain, rev. of *ECT* VII in *Chronique d'Egypte* 37 (1962) 297-300; Thomas George Allen, rev. of *ECT* VII in *JNES* 22 (1963) 133-137; Dieter Müller, rev. of *ECT* VII in *BibO* 20 (1963), 246-250; Paul Barguet, "Essai d'Interprétation du Livre des Deux Chemins," *Rd'E* 21 (1969) 7-17; and L. H. Lesko, "Some Observations on the Composition of the *Book of Two Ways*," *JAOS* 91 (1971) 30-43.

[10] Cf. L. H. Lesko, *op. cit.*, 41-42.

[11] Hermann Grapow, *op. cit.*, p. 49.

[12] The fact that Osiris is associated with several of these goals may be related to the fact that the identities and attributes of various other local gods of the dead were assigned to him. Thus Osiris who was originally a god of Busiris became god of Abydos and was assigned the attributes of the original god

of Abydos, Khentyimentiu. In one section of the Book of Two Ways Osiris is associated with Rosetaw, and it seems that the texts probably referred to Sokar, the god of the Giza necropolis, originally.

DESCRIPTION, TRANSLATION

AND NOTES

SECTION I

The introduction to the longer group represented by versions A and B includes spells 1029-1035, while the introduction to the shorter group, version C, is contained in spell 1131.

In the longer group, the <u>Book of Two Ways</u> begins with a description of the rising sun-god, Re, who, while proceeding from the eastern horizon in the shrine of his bark, is addressed by the deceased.

CT 1029^a (1)

A,B^b ^{252}May trembling befall the eastern horizon of the sky at the voice of Nut as she clears the ways for Re,^{c} before the Great One,^{d} so that he may make the circuit.^{e}
^{253}Raise yourself, O Re, Raise yourself,^{f} O you who are in your shrine, that you may lap up the winds,^{g} ^{254}that you may swallow the vertebrae, that you may spit out^h the day, and that you may breathe^i Maat.^{j} May the Followers go around^k when the^l bark travels to Nut.^{m} ^{255}May the Great Ones^n quiver^o at your voice.^{p} May you count your^q bones. May you pull together your limbs.^{r} May you turn your face to the beautiful West as you come^s anew^t every day, ^{256}because^u you are that^v image of gold^w wearing the ⌜radiant⌝^{x} locks.^{y} As for the sky and earth, they fall before you^z trembling because^{aa} you circle^{ab} ever anew every day.^{257} The^{ac} horizon rejoices; there is joy at your tow rope.^{ad}

^{a}Cf. de Buck <u>ECT</u>, VII, 252ff. The superlinear numbers in the translation give these page numbers. The parenthetical number after the CT spell number refers to the key number on the plans of the bottoms of the coffins which are found at the back of de Buck's edition.

^{b}Version A occurs on B3C, B12C, B13C, B6C, B4L, B2Bo, B4C, B4Bo, and B9C. Version B occurs on B1L, B2L, B3L, B2P, and B1C. The text also occurs in <u>Book of the Dead</u> chapter 133a.

^{c}B2Bo and B9C omit the suffix pronoun <u>s</u>; "The ways were cleared for. . ..."

11

[d] "Great One" seems to repeat Re in a not uncommon form of doublet.

[e] Or "when he circles."

[f] Version B omits this second "raise yourself."

[g] Version B adds "that you may swallow the north winds."

[h] Version B and Book of the Dead have ibt "⸢snare⸣," cf. Wb. I, 65, 1, for ibt.t "Vogelfalle."

[i] B13C has snsn; probably "breathe," but possibly "mingle with."

[j] "Order" or "Truth" is often personified as a goddess in these texts.

[k] Version B and the BD have pšn "separate."

[l] B12C, B13C, B6C, B4L, B2Bo and probably B9C have "your bark."

[m] The goddess of the sky.

[n] B2Bo and B9C have "your Great Ones." For wrw, B2L has wiš (sic!).

[o] B1C has nm "travel" for nmnm.

[p] "At your voice" is omitted in B9C.

[q] B6C omits k "your."

[r] B2P has "your bones have been counted; your limbs have been pulled together."

[s] Cf. Polotsky, "Tenses," p. 5 for these circumstantial forms. iwy, iy, and iw occur here.

[t] B-version has "ever anew."

[u] B1L, B2L, B3L, and B2P omit n.

[v] B12C, B13C, B6C, B4L, B2Bo, B9C, and B2L add nfr, "that beautiful image."

[w] B-version apparently has šsmt "malachite."

[x] Written itnwt with bookroll determinative in B3C, without a determinative elsewhere in version A. B13C, B6C, and B4L omit the final t and may be equal to itnw, "opposing" locks, cf. Wb. I, 146, 1. Version B seems to have "⸢radiant⸣." An earlier use of the verb referred to in Wb. I, 145, 12 is proposed. Also possible is Allen's rendering in BD, p. 218, note i: "bearing the pates of the disks."

[y] Written smiw and usually rendered "temple" or "pate," cf. Allen, BD, p. 218, and Lefebvre, Tableau des parties du corps humain, ("Supplément" to ASAE, Cahier No. 17) 1952. For the meaning "locks" cf. Wb. IV, 122, 5, and Von Deines and Westendorf, WMT, II, 749-750.

[z] The words ti hr.sn n.k do not occur in version B.

[aa] B4L omits n.

[ab] For dbn, B3L has wbn with walking legs determinative for "stride briskly," "rise" (?).

[ac] B9C adds "Maat rejoices at your approach."

Section I   13

^{ad}B12C pluralizes "horizon" and "tow rope." Version B adds the rubric, "SPELL FOR SAILING IN THE GREAT BARK OF RE."

This first spell alone illustrates the frequent and consistent textual differences between versions A and B. B1C agrees with version B throughout, but B9C generally follows version A and is occasionally unique. Since these two sources elsewhere show affinities to one or the other of these two versions, they have been designated as version A-B.

The reference to "tow rope" in spell 1029 is notable because of later references to oars and rowing. The rubric added at the end of the B-version would better be the heading for the next spell since the deceased in CT 1029 is not yet with Re.

CT 1030 (2)

A^a 258The starry host^b is in Heliopolis, the sun people in Babylon, because of^c the birth^d of its thousand gods to him who has bound on his headband and has grasped^e his steering oar. 259 I go down^f with them to the ⌜lotus-prowed boat⌝^{g} at the dockyard of the gods, that I may take a bark^h therefrom, two lotuses^i at its^j ends,^{k} that^l 260I may sail in it^m with (him) as "Monkey-heart,"^{n} and 261 that I may act as pilot^o in it to that^p district of Nut, to the stairway^q of Mercury.^{r}

B^s 258The starry host is in Heliopolis, the sun people in Babylon, O you who have given birth to a thousand gods, who have bound on your headband and who have hewn^t your steering oar. 259May I be judged with them at the rigging-lofts^u of^v the dockyard^w of the gods, that I may take therefrom a bark with lotus^x at its ends, that I may go forth in it^y to the sky, 260that I may sail in it to Nut, that I may sail in it with Re,^{z} and that I may sail in it with^{aa} (him) in "Monkey-heart"^{ab} 261 on that district of Nut at that stairway of Mercury.
SPELL FOR SAILING IN THE GREAT BARK OF RE.^{ac}

aVersion A occurs in B3C, B4C, B12C, B13C, B6C, B4L, B2Bo, B4Bo, and B9C. The text also occurs in BD 136a.

bAs Allen BD, p. 220. Cf. CDME, p. 184 for ḥȝbȝs "starry sky"; also Blackman in JEA 21 (1935) 5, note 3.

cOr for the rendering of n "at the time of" cf. ECT, I 196 c; James, Hekanakhte, Letter II, 32: and perhaps Urk, IV, 765, 10.

dB12C omits n mswt.

eTo account for the additional n in B3C read "and to him who has grasped." B9C with adze determinative of nḏr has "and has hewn."

fB9C has wdꜥ as does version B.

gWritten sšnt with bark determinative. B12C has nšmt "sacred bark of Osiris."

hB3C omits ỉm "therefrom."

iCf. Wb. III, 218. B9C has [n]hȝ. For a discussion of hȝwy and nhȝ meaning "recurved" cf. Allen, BD, p. 221, note f.

jB4Bo omits the suffix pronoun f.

kB12C, B13C, and B4L have r tp.f "at its tip," instead of r tpwy.f(y).

lB2Bo, B4Bo, and B9C add before this, "that I may go forth in it to the sky."

mB4L omits ỉm.f while B9C adds r pt "to the sky" after it.

nGf-ỉb, cf. Allen, BD, p. 222, note i.

oWd, cf. CDME, p. 74.

pB12C omits tw.

qB3C and B9C add pw, "to that stairway."

rSbg, cf. Wb, IV, 95, 8 for later occurrences of the word.

sVersion B occurs in B1L, B2L, B3L, B1C, and B2P.

tB2L, B1C, and B2P have "grasped."

uWritten sšnt with plural strokes and also with house determinative in B1C. Cf. Allen, BD, p. 221, note e, and Wb. IV, 293.

vB2L has nwȝ for n.

wPlural in B1C.

xOr "recurved."

yB1L omits f.

zInstead of these last two clauses, B1L has "and sail with Re."

aaB2L substitutes r "to" for ḥnꜥ.

abWith a ship determinative in the B-version, this is apparently the name of a bark. The determinative is uncertain in B3L, and, with m omitted here, it has "that I may sail in it with monkey-heart."

acB1C adds "EVERY DAY."

Section I 15

Just as with "Re" and "Great One" in 1029, spell 1030 apparently begins with another duplication since "sun-people" are usually of Heliopolis, not nearby Babylon. The lotus-prowed boat which the deceased chooses, though not depicted, would seem to be the simple type which Nebseni is supposed to be rowing in chapter 110 of his <u>Book of the Dead</u> (Budge, <u>BD</u>, p. 319). But if the deceased is actually choosing the solar bark on which he also appears in these texts, the bark might be that of spell 1128's vignette which also could be lotus-prowed similar to Ani's of the aforementioned <u>Book of the Dead</u> scene (Budge (<u>BD</u>, p. 322). The substitution in B12C of Osiris' bark seems unwarranted here. The stairway, which is also not illustrated here, calls to mind the stairway on the bark in the "Field of Offerings" vignette from chapter 110 of the <u>Book of the Dead</u>. The rubric of version B could again belong to the next spell, which is properly CT 1033. Reference to the daily accompaniment of Re occurs here only in B1C.

The last lines of the last spell (1130) of the <u>Book of Two Ways</u> on B3C were placed in vacant space near the beginning of the "book" and de Buck designated these lines as a separate spell (1031) in the edition. CT 1031 is given below in its proper place at the end of spell 1130 in version A.

The labels found on the borders enclosing CT 1033 are called 1032, and they refer to the gods who travel on the solar bark. These gods are named later in CT 1128. It is this "entourage of flame" that is addressed at the beginning of spell 1033.

CT 1032 (3)

A,B[a] [262] Entourage of flame. Entourage of flame. Entourage of flame. Entourage of flame.

[a] In B2L, B3L, B1C, and B2P the heading occurs on each of the four red borders of the rectangle which encloses CT 1033. On B9C it occurs only once across the top of the rectangle, and on B2Bo it occurs on each of the vertical sides.

CT 1033 (4)

A[a] [263]This flame which burns[b] against[c] you is that which is around Re, that which is bound together around him. Be fearful! A lord of storm is the Re-bark. Join the flame! [264]I have come hither with "⌜Wiped-face⌝."[d] I have seen the one who has attained Maat [265]fallen through the agency of[e] those splendid of form who are in the bend of the sacred lake, the companions of[f] the ⌜reed-dwellers⌝[g] of the lake[h] of reeds. [266]I have seen them there.[i] We shall hand them over.[j] Their great ones are in joy; their little ones are in happiness. [267]Make way for me at the prow of his[k] bark. Shine[l] in his disk, be effective in his[m] soul, and rise up[n] in front of his Uraei [268]when he partakes of offerings as the lord of Maat. [269]I have accumulated[o] what is injured in him. [270]I have brought Maat to him that he may live on it. Go, go! Come, come! Tell the condition of his[p] father in Nun [271]and convey his voice at evening. I have come, [273]bringing[q] Apopis to him,[r] and I have spat upon his wounds for him. Make way for me that I may pass by.[s] [274]I am the greatest of the gods. Come, pass by,[t] that your bark[u] may be rowed along, O lord,[v] Perception. You are heir of the Great One. [275]⌜Dampen⌝[w] the flame; extinguish the fire.[x] Make way for me. It is the one who unites[y] them that causes the horizon to approach me.[z] [276]I have passed the great ones. I have instructed[aa] the ⌜Westerner⌝[ab] who is in his bark. I have traversed the entourage of flame [277]which is around the lord of those who wear the sidelock.
Pass by, says Horakhte, that you may govern[ac] the bark, the eye of your father.

B[ad] [263]This flame which ⌜burns⌝[ae] against ⟨you⟩[af] is that which is around Re, that which is bound together around him. Be fearful when the bark of Re rages, and join what is sacred. [264]I have come hither[ag] with "⌜Wiped-face⌝" in the bend of the sacred lake.[ah] I have seen the one who has attained Maat [265]fallen among[ai] those holy of form who are in ⌜sarcophagi⌝.[aj] Bountiful it is,[ak] the lake of reeds. [266]I have seen there. We shall (go) to them {them}[al] Their great ones are in joy; their little ones are in

happiness. ²⁶⁷Make way for me at the prow of the bark of the one whose disk shines and who is effective in his soul^(am) that I may rise up in front of his Uraei ²⁶⁸when he partakes of^(an) the offerings while being embraced as the lord of Maat.^(ao)
⌜WHAT IS THIS? (IT IS) A SHRINE⌝.^(ap)
I am the one who circles^(aq) the Great Bulls, ²⁶⁹the son of the kite (Isis) of Osiris. He has testified concerning his father, the lord of those things which are within. I have removed what is injured in him. ²⁷⁰⌜SUBSTITUTION⌝.^(ar) I have brought Tefnut to him that he may live on it.^(as) GO! COME!^(at) (REPEAT). TELL HIS CONDITION!^(au) ²⁷¹EXHIBIT MAAT TO THE ALL-LORD.^(av) GO! MAKE INVOCATION AT EVENING. I have come, ²⁷²bringing to him^(aw) the two jaws which were in Rosetaw, bringing to him the spine which was in Heliopolis, and I have united unto him his throng.^(ax) ²⁷³I have opposed Apopis,^(ay) and I have spat upon the wounds for him.^(az) Make way for me that I may pass among you. ²⁷⁴I am the greatest of the gods. COME, PASS BY, ROW THE BARK OF THE LORD, PERCEPTION, ONWARDS.^(ba) YOU ARE HEIR OF THE GREAT ONE.^(bb) ²⁷⁵⌜Dampen⌝ the flame that he may extinguish^(bc) the fire. Make way for me. It is their Illuminers whom the horizon admits,^(bd) ²⁷⁶that I may pass the Great Ones, after I have ⌜instructed⌝ the ⌜Westerner⌝^(be) who is in his bark, and after I have traversed the entourage of fire ²⁷⁷which is around the lord of those who wear the sidelock.
PASS BY US, SAYS HORUS, THE LORD, AND PREPARE THE BARK "YOUR EYE (IS) THE FATHER."
²⁷⁸SPELL FOR PASSING THE FLAMING ENTOURAGE OF THE ⌜CABIN⌝^(bf) OF RE'S BARK.^(bg)

---

^(a)Version A occurs in B3C, B4C, B12C, B13C, B6C, B4L, B1Bo, B2Bo, and B4Bo. B9C has affinities to both versions A and B. The text also occurs in BD 136b.

^(b)B12C has wbdt, cf. Wb. I, 297, 1; B1Bo has wbdt and B6C and B4L apparently have bdt as variants of wbdt. B2Bo and B4Bo have bht and B9C has bht as variants of Bhh, cf. Wb. I, 472, 1.

^(c)B4L omits r.

^(d)Sk-hr, or, "destroyed of face."

^(e)M-ꜥ, "⌜among⌝" or "from" are also possible.

^{f}Or "and." B9C follows the A-version here.

^{g}Swtyw, "those of the reeds."

^{h}B1Bo has nbw, "lords," for š.

^{i}B12C, B4L, and B4Bo omit im.

^{j}Perhaps "deliver" or "allot them," cf. Simpson, Papyrus Reisner I, Boston, 1963, p. 83. Emend n in B3C to r as in the other mss. The sentence is omitted in B9C.

^{k}B4Bo has "your."

^{l}B12C adds suffixes, "that I may shine in his disk, that I may be effective in his soul, and that I may rise up in front of his Uraei."

^{m}B4Bo has "your."

^{n}B2Bo and B4Bo have "that I may rise up in front of his Uraei."

^{o}Cf. Baer, "An Eleventh Dynasty Farmer's Letters to his Family," JAOS, LXXXIII (1963) p. 5, note 22, "gather" or "pile up." B-version has wdꜥ, "removed," and this seems to fit the context better.

^{p}B12C has k, "your."

^{q}Cf. Polotsky, "Tenses," p. 5, for the circumstantial sdm.n.f of in.

^{r}B4Bo omits "to him."

^{s}B6C adds im.s, "on it."

^{t}B12C omits r of the particle rk, "Come and pass by."

^{u}B4C has iwr, a strange writing of wi̯.

^{v}B13C has Rꜥ for nb, "Re and Perception."

^{w}Apparently written id for i̯d related to i̯dt, "dew," "water." The usual rendering, "cense," does not fit the context.

^{x}B3C repeats sdt, "flame" instead of ht.

^{y}Written i̯bh, but perhaps it should be wbh, "who illumines." Note wbnw in B-version.

^{z}Or, "It is the one who unites them that the horizon lets approach me." Cf. Gunn, Studies in Egyptian Syntax, Paris 1924, p. 59 (6). B6C has "that causes me to approach the horizon." B6C also adds r before i̯ht, while B4Bo adds m. B9C repeats sꜥ of sꜥr by dittography.

^{aa}Or "testified concerning."

^{ab}Imy-wr, cf. Sethe, Die aegyptischen Ausdrücke für rechts und links, (NAWG Göttingen, 1922, pp. 231-232.

^{ac}For hrp, B12C substitutes ꜥhꜥ, "stand up."

^{ad}Version B occurs in B1L, B2L, B1C, and B2P. B9C has affinities to versions A and B.

^{ae}Written i̯bht, apparently a variant of bhh, cf. Wb, I, 472, 1.

^{af}Generally written rn.t, but, since "your (fem.) name" has no antecedent, it seems best to emend to r.tn as in version A.

Section I

ᵃᵍB1L has a disk determinative, "today"? B2L omits the word.

ᵃʰB2P omits š. B9C follows the B-version in adding the phrase.

ᵃⁱOn m "with," "among" cf. Schenkel, <u>Grundformen mittelägyptischer Sätze</u>, (Münchner ägyptologische Studien, 7). Berlin, 1965, p. 7. B3L omits m.

ᵃʲAssuming that dbȝt (<u>Wb</u>, V, 561, 12) is wrongly determined here, but note the proper writings of "sarcophagi" on the same coffins, <u>ECT</u>, VII 455 a.

ᵃᵏDe Buck notes that an r in B2L was canceled. If the r were an oral mistake, the vulture is indeed the particle ȝ and not the tȝw of A-version.

ᵃˡPerhaps a dittography repeated from B3L or its source, or possibly supplies the "them" missing in the preceding sentence (from split columns of original?).

ᵃᵐB1C has "that I may shine in his disk, that I may be effective in his soul."

ᵃⁿB1C substitutes dbȝ for smȝ and with the suffix on sbh seems to have "he repays the accounts so that I may be embraced."

ᵃᵒB3L has "lord of the two Maats," and B1C has "lord of the Uraei of the two Maats." B1L omitting nb has "being embraced in truth."

ᵃᵖWritten m py in B2L, B3L, B1C, and B2P; <u>my py</u> in B1L. Also possible: "WHAT IS THIS, THE SHRINE?" or "WHO IS THIS, WHAT IS THE SHRINE?" cf. <u>ECT</u>, IV, 77 c.

ᵃᑫB9C has "I am the evil one of the Great Bulls."

ᵃʳȝIdnt, from ȝdn "serve instead of," cf. <u>CDME</u> p. 35.

ᵃˢB1L and B1C have ȝm.f; B2L and B2P have ȝm.s; B3L omits the phrase.

ᵃᵗB2L and B2P omit mȝ.

ᵃᵘOr "SAY TO THE FATHER." (?).

ᵃᵛOr "LORD, ATUM." B9C has "TO THE LORD, RE-ATUM."

ᵃʷB2L has "to you."

ᵃˣB2P has "I united unto him those who are in Heliopolis. I united unto him [his] throng."

ᵃʸB9C, B3L, and B1C add "for him."

ᵃᶻB9C has m nspw for nspw. B2P adds the particle ȝw to psg.n.ȝ making it independent.

ᵇᵃB2L and B1C have "that the bark of the lord of Perception may be rowed onwards."

ᵇᵇFeminine in all but B3L.

ᵇᶜB2L and B3L omit the suffix and so continue the imperative.

ᵇᵈOr "Way has been made for me by their illuminers whom the horizon has admitted."

^{be}B1L has imy-wrt for imy-wr; B1C has imy-wrw, "⌜Westerners⌝;" and B9C has wrw, "the Great Ones."

^{bf}Or "⌜SHRINE⌝," written r-iwȝ, determined with a red crown, also a shrine or wood.

^{bg}B1C adds "EVERY DAY."

The beginning of this spell seems to refer to those deceased who become stars in the "house of Maat" according to the Thoth tradition. The Thoth tradition is found in section VI, spells 1088-1098 and is apparently resumed again in CT 1115-1116. The deceased seeks a place at the prow of Re's bark and joins the "entourage of flame." Nun is the watery abyss and Apopis is the serpent intent upon devouring the sun-bark. The deceased identifies himself as the greatest god, and, in version B, as the "son of the kite," he is clearly Horus. The instruction he gives would seem to make him hrp wiȝ or pilot as in Amduat (cf. Hornung, Amduat, II, 22, no. 51). The bark, which is named here, is rowed and not towed. Nothing is added to the intelligibility of the spell by the rubricized gloss and "substitution" in version B.

CT 1034 (5)

A,B ^{a} [278]On your faces, ⌜mysterious⌝^{b} serpents. Let me pass. ^{279}I am a mighty one,^{c} the lord of those of might.^{d} I am a dignitary^e of Re,^{f} the lord of Maat, the begetter of Uto. The protection of Re is my protection.^{g} ^{280}He^h has travelled around the Field of Offerings^i belonging to me.^{j} I am Re, a greater god than you,^{k}^{281}who counts^l his enneads in^m giving offerings.^{n}
THE GUIDE OF THE WAYS OF ROSETAW.^{o}

CT 1035 (6)

B ^{282}I have passed the ways of Rosetaw^p which are on water and land.^{q} These are the ways of Osiris.^{r} They are on the edge of the sky. As for any person who knows this spell for going down by them,^{s} he is a holy god^t in the suite of Thoth.^{u} Moreover, he can go down to^v any sky ^{283}into which^w he desires to go down. But as for him who does^x not know how to pass^y on^z those ways, he shall be taken^{aa}

by a ⌜stroke⌝[ab] of death which[ac] is ordained, being a nonentity[ad] who has no Maat forever.

[a]Version A occurs in B3C, B4C, B12C, B13C, B6C, B4L, B1Bo, B2Bo, and B4Bo. B1L, B2L, B3L, B2P, B1C, and B9C have version B. Cf. BD 136b.

[b]Or "serpents of the Beyond," cf. ECT, I 182 e, and Schott, Die Schrift der verborgenen Kammer, (NAWG, 1958, no. 4), pp. 348-349.

[c]B6C omits wsr, "I am lord of those of might."

[d]A nisbe on wsrwt; or "those who have necks," perhaps referring to "posts," cf. Barguet, Le Livre des Morts, Paris 1967, p. 145, note 6, and Zandee, Death as an Enemy, p. 225, "torturing-post." Cf. also the middle register of the sixth division of the Book of Gates. B12C, B6C, and B4L have "lord of might."

[e]For a discussion of the term sꜥḥ with the meaning "transfigured spirit" cf. Lichtheim, "The High Steward Akhamenru," JNES, VII (1948) 176.

[f]B1Bo has Rꜥ pw, "He is Re."

[g]B3C and B4C omit "is my protection." B1Bo has "My protection is her (Uto's) protection and the protection of Re."

[h]B9C omits the particle mtn. B12C, B13C, and B6C omit the enclitic particle m.

[i]B6C, B4L, B9C, B2L, B3L, and B2P have "the Field of Ḥetep." B3C, B6C, B2Bo, and B9C have shty (dual!).

[j]Cf. Gardiner, "Two Employments of the Independent Pronouns," JEA, XX (1934) 15-17, and Edel, Alt. Gr. I, §368. The break in B3C seems too short for nnk of most other mss. B1Bo, B4Bo, and B9C omit nnk, and B3L has nn in error.

[k]B9C has "I am [a greater god] than you." B12C has "I am Re, a god whom you cause to ascend," because of the similarity of hieratic signs.

[l]Or "when he counts." Perhaps ip should be "pays" here, cf. Eloquent Peasant, B1, 178.

[m]Written mm for m in all B-version mss. though not in B9C. If this is not another dittography repeated from B3L, other examples of mm for m occur in ECT, I 157 d, and 158 d.

[n]B6C has "as one who gives ⌜your⌝ offerin[!gs]."

[o]Omitted in B1Bo and B-version mss. Spell 1036 follows version A. Rubrics occur in B3C, B4L, B12C, and B13C. "Guide" is feminine sšmt in B13C, B6C, B4L, and B2Bo.

[p]B9C begins with "Guide of the ways in Rosetaw."

[q]B2P has "which are on water and which are on land."

[r]B2P seems to have "These are the ways which ⌜come to⌝ me," but perhaps iwr is a writing of wsir as in B2L.

[s]B9C has r.s "to it." B2L, B1C, and B2P are rubricized from ir to the end of the spell.

^tB9C has "He is himself a god," ds.f (with f reversed) for dsr, with mm for m of predication.

^uB9C adds iw.f, "He is in the suite of Thoth."

^vFor r, B3L has m, "in."

^wFor im.s, B9C has r.s.

^xOr "is unable to." For sdm.n.f after iwty as a present tense, cf. Edel. Alt. Gr. §1068. B9C has rh.f and adds r pn n, "But as for him who does not know this spell for passing."

^yFeminine t occurs on sw₰ in B1L. B3L omits sw₰.

^zB2L and B9C omit hr.

^{aa}As in B1C. Very likely it.f was also written in B9C. Other mss. omitted it.f.

^{ab}Written 'b₰, it could also be "the fetters," cf. Zandee, Death as an Enemy, p. 126.

^{ac}B1C adds m before s₰yt, "as that which is ordained."

^{ad}Taking swt of B1L, B2L, and B3L as independent pronoun used instead of the dependent pronoun, sw, which occurs in B1C. It could also be a particle restricting the phrase, "But as a nonentity," cf. James, Hekanakhte, p. 28.

Spells 1034 and 1035 give the raison d'être of the guidebook which follows and they present the gods who figure importantly in it. In spell 1034 the deceased addresses the demons who will be encountered on the forthcoming ways. By presenting his credentials and especially by identifying himself with the sun-god, Re, the deceased hopes to intimidate the demons into letting him pass. The brief reference to the deceased as a functionary of Re is elaborated upon in one whole section below as is also his relationship to Osiris in the Field of Offerings. Spell 1035 seems to be an expansion in the B-version of the rubric in version A of spell 1034, but its function is also to connect the third tradition, concerning Thoth, to the two above and thus help unify the whole. The deceased who knows this spell can move about in the sky as he likes, while one who does not know how to pass on the ways will perish.

Version C begins with its own brief introduction, proceeds through the ground plan of a building or buildings in section II, includes the central map of sections III-IV, and ends rather abruptly after a short version of the two ways which follows the central map on all versions in section V.

Section I

Spell 1131 apparently addresses Osiris rather than Re, and the whole is notably more earthy in its description than the preceding introduction to versions A and B. The deceased has come to see Osiris, live beside him, and rot beside him. The rubric tells the deceased what he must do in order to reach his goal. The book provides the gatekeeper's names (words or speech) in writing, and, if the deceased knows the names, he can easily pass the gatekeepers and reach his goal which is to sit beside the great god (Osiris). While the introductions to the two groups or sources both state the rewards or punishments for knowledge or ignorance of succeeding spells, this is evidently put in very different terms.

CT 1131 (1')

C^a ^{472}Hail to you, my father^b and the two companions^c in your beautiful field,^{d} lord^e of those who gave to the defiant^f your putrefaction in it. It lightens more than the sky in your soul when Re stands in the midst of the sky to lead his keepers. It is on the smells that he, Re-Atum, turns his back. The lock (of hair) was cut off^g and the eye which the pellet^h in^i its socket^j sealed. May the pellet^k which went forth from you live having covered^l the head of a nail. (As) the fly flies,^{m} Osiris lives, who pulls together the Great One (repeat), the flood-waters and the sacred cows. I am a creator^n and a wise man. ^{473}I am a creator, one who raises (his) father. I created^o the Great One (male) and the Great One (female). I created the great ⌜green⌝ ^{p} and the great flood-waters. I am the ⌜defiant one⌝ ^{q} of Khnum who takes away enmity.^{r} This is the creator who cuts off the ⌜. . .⌝^{s} of the house. I have come that I may see Osiris, live beside him, and rot beside him. I resemble you. I am your image. A PICTURE OF THE DOUBLE DOORS OF THE HORIZON^t WHEN THEY PLACED A SEAL ON THE GODS. THESE ARE THE NAMES OF THEIR KEEPERS WHICH ARE IN WRITING. INDEED THIS IS THEIR FORM ENTIRELY. AS FOR ANY PERSON WHO DOES NOT KNOW THEIR WORDS, HE FALLS INTO THE TRAPS^v OF THE VALLEY^w THERE. THEIR^x NAMES HAVE BEEN WRITTEN,^{y} THEY BEING BESIDE THOSE [EVIL ONES].^{z} ^{474}AS FOR ANY PERSON WHO WILL KNOW THEIR WORDS,

HE WILL PASS BY THERE. HE WILL SIT BESIDE THE GREAT GOD IN ANY PLACE WHERE HE IS.^{aa} HE WILL FEAR HIM HIMSELF. HE IS ENTIRELY PERFECT^{ab} AND SPIRIT. AS FOR ANY PERSON WHO WILL KNOW, HE WILL NOT PERISH FOREVER. THEY WILL PLACE A SEAL ON HIM LIKE EVERY GOD FOR WHOM THEY DO IT WITH ALL THE GODS.

^{a}Version C occurs in B1Be, B1P, and B5C.

^{b}This apparently refers to Osiris.

^{c}Rhwy can also refer to Horus and Seth, but here it is probably a reference to Re and Thoth representing the sun and moon.

^{d}The Field of Offerings.

^{e}B1P has nb, but B1Be omits it. B5C is illegible.

^{f}Written btn, see btn, Wb. I, 486, 1.

^{g}Hdk, cf. Wb. III, 206, 1.

^{h}Written tʒ, cf. Wb. V, 341.

^{i}Or "of." Written with n in all three mss. A verb nbʒbʒ? cf. Wb. II, 243, 14.

^{j}Bʒbʒ, cf. Wb. I, 419.

^{k}As in note h, or is tʒ, "fledgling," cf. Wb. V, 339.

^{l}Sʿfn is the causative of ʿfn, Wb. I, 183.

^{m}Written ipʒ for pʒ in B1P.

^{n}Or "potter."

^{o}Or "fashioned."

^{p}De Buck suggested that this uncertain sign be read wʒd.

^{q}See note f above. Here the word is btnn or perhaps bw tnn since the b is followed by a stroke.

^{r}Rkkt, cf. rk, Wb. II, 456.

^{s}Ynʒsf (?)

^{t}Cf. Zandee, Death as an Enemy, pp. 161-2 and 258 for his translation of parts of this rubric.

^{u}B1P ends here, and, since B5C became illegible just before the rubric began, the text continues from B1Be alone.

^{v}Written innwt, the word is certainly related to intnt (Wb. I, 102) and int, intt (CDME, p. 24) from inn (Wb. I, 97). Zandee, Death as an Enemy, suggests "traps" or "snares."

^{w}Int for an obvious play on words.

^{x}A few signs must be restored here, but the meaning is clear from the signs that survive and traces that can be reasonably well identified.

^{y}Hʒb "send" can be "write" with reference to letters. The extension to this particular situation is required by the context.

^{z}N[bdw] can probably be restored here.

^{aa}Written bw nb ntf ʒm.

^{ab}Or "EQUIPPED" ʿpr.

SECTION II

Spell 1132 begins section II, which consists of the spells found in a number of compartments which lead to the ground plan of a building. The section takes up most of the upper register on the three C-version coffins involved. The texts here are generally the most difficult of the book. In addition to corruptions and unknown words, there are numerous allusions to things that we cannot understand. The texts are included here for the little that we can get from them and also for comparison with the other sections.
In CT 1132 there is a gate to be passed, and the deceased identifies himself with Nun, the watery abyss. He tells the demon keepers that he knows them from their pictures, probably because he has this illustrated book. This spell sets the pattern for those following through 1139. In most of these the deceased claims to have come from some special place for some purpose.

CT 1132 (2')

C^a [474]The gate of flaming-front, hidden back,^{b} in which there is a man^c who is bound. It is in the firmament with the sun^d ⌜for a duration⌝.^{e} I am Nun, lord of darkness. ^{475}I have come that I may have power over the way and that his faces may be afraid of me. I am the one who is heavy for you on your two shoulders, who ⌜. . .⌝^{f} for you the two shoulders ⌜when I said^g that you reached the^h father⌝ . I have come here from Heliopolis that I may ⟨be crowned⟩^{i} with the Mighty One, that I may see the bull of Heliopolis in their form, that I may see water^j in darkness. Say to them. I know them by their pictures. I saw their mother's delivery. May I draw for you ⌜among⌝^{k} them the name of N., bull of Heliopolis, that they may illumine me ⌜inside⌝.^{l}

^aVersion C occurs in B1Be, B1P, and B5C.

^bFor other translations of parts of this spell cf. Zandee, Death, pp. 28-29 and 115, also Kees, Totenglauben, p. 290.

^cSo in B1P and B5C, but B1Be probably has more missing.

^dOr, "it is a marvel in the day."

^eHr ꣿwt.

^fNshwh. For tfꣿ below, Kees suggested that we read ꣿtf. It is very possible that signs have become disordered elsewhere in these texts. If this is the case here, we could have snhw followed by hnꜥ "which were bound together with you."

^gIf this is fd and not dd then we could suggest "the two shoulders which removed for you its strength."

^hOr "my."

ⁱOr another unknown verb written tfꣿ.

^jB5C and B1P have "my water," or should it be "within me?" cf. ECT, VII 475 m.

^kM for mm.

^lWritten mw for m-hnw.

In spell 1133 the deceased says that he will show the way on which he passes, and he identifies himself with other deities.

CT 1133 (3')

C^a   476 I show this way on which I pass. I am Usernen, lord of secrets. I am mightiest of all ⌜Tjennut-gods⌝.^b I am the squalor of the lungs. As for Shu he passes by the liver on the sledge.^c Mine is my father.

^aThis occurs in B1Be, B1P. and B5C.

^bI.e., Osiris, cf. Wb. V, 382, 1-4. As de Buck noted, the word could also be rnnwt "I am rich in joy," but, with the god-determinative followed by plural strokes and nb, this seems much less likely.

^cWritten tp tm, or, "first of all."

The gatekeeper of the mansion of "Numerous-faces" in CT 1134 is a perfect spirit. The mansion is probably indicated by the dark wall that encloses spells 1132-1134.

Section II
CT 1134 (4')

$^{C\,a}$ Open to me and then I shall sleep. Open to me and I shall be protected^b from them.^{c} It is a perfect spirit who guards the gate of the mansion of Numerous-faces.^{d} I have come after I travelled^e the waters.^{f} ^{477}I moved about until you called,^{g} and I passed by the shoulders of Osiris. He knows that mine are these who are in the gates, their guardians. I am a lord of travelling who was not opposed afterward. I went after, my face not having been around you,^{h} like ⌈Atjen⌉^{i} and the two companions. Mine is travelling here. He causes that I be a mummy like the one who raises himself. I am more excellent than the lord of places when I see^j that he makes them in their form. ^{478}I have come here from Dep that I may see the growing plant,^{k} and that I may see it^l in my day. The mansions belong to his face. My head will be mine, my arms will be mine, and my legs will be mine. I am Wrapped-up^m who is in Dep, Dep^n which is on him having become him.^{o} I am he. I am Wrapped-up who is in darkness.

^{a}This version occurs in B1Be, B1P and B5C.

^{b}A causative of mk is proposed.

^{c}The whole beginning of this spell could also be translated "Open to her since further she opened the protection from them." There is, however, no antecedent for the feminine pronouns, and hr should be non-enclitic.

^{d}"Numerous-faces" could also be the name of the perfect spirit used in apposition. Zandee, Death, p. 129, used this statement from this spell, and he suggested "with many faces." I have taken it as a name because of the determinative in B5C.

^{e}B1Be adds a word that looks like dwm with walking legs determinative. Perhaps this is mnmn ⌈"moving about." Cf. Wb. II, 64-65, for Gardiner's sign N26 used later in the 19th dynasty for mn.

^{f}For hnt cf. Wb. III, 105, 4. Caminos, Literary Fragments, pl. 1, 2, 4, has "swampy lake."

^{g}This assumes another metathesis, ʿtš for šʿt. Otherwise "I moved about (cf. note e, above) since your lake was given (?)".

^{h}Or, "I went behind my face, not being around you."

^{i}Written ꜣtn, for ỉtn "sun-disk"?

^{j}Cf. Polotsky, "Tenses," p. 20 for a reference to this verb.

^{k}B1Be has sw "him", or "it" for sm.
^{l}B1Be omits sw.
^{m}Or "Headcloth" ⸗fnwt.
^{n}B1Be does not repeat "Dep."
^{o}Or, "having come to be from him."

Spells 1135-1139 are set off as another group with a red "flaming" wall surrounding them on B1Be. The spells are each contained in separate compartments and there are demons and double flaming doors in all but the center compartment. In CT 1135 the deceased lists his accomplishments so that he may pass. He not only came from Abydos but is "foremost of Abydos."

CT 1135 (5')

C^a ^{479}The souls of Nekhen.^{b} The Seizers, the keepers of his limbs in rage. They protect Contrary-face.^{c}
Flame. Flame.
Hail to you who seize his lands for him, O keepers of limbs in rage. I am the Nekhenite who has borne your snakes. I am the torch which is in you. May I pass with Shu in Nun. I am the one who satisfied his heart after the mistress. I am the one who will restore the sky to order. I am the one who will have power over darkness. More mighty is the striking force (of God)^d than that of the Mighty-one. ^{480}Mine are those who are possessors of requirements. I am his protection in darkness, the Terrible-one who went forth from his eye. I have come here from Abydos, after I found his water, that the snakes may go down ⟨to⟩ ^{e} their holes in a boat.^{f} He goes down applauding the state of affairs before Nekhnekh^g and their shoulders. I am foremost of Abydos, when he has bound^h his horn in fighting. Mine is the clean way.

^{a}This occurs in B1Be, B1P, and B5C.
^{b}This heading is found only on B5C.
^{c}Cf. also ECT, I 208 a, and VII 370 k. The epithet or name is discussed in Wb. II, 290, 15-18; Blackman JEA 5 (1918) 26, n. 7; and Zandee, Death, p. 109.
^{d}İt is personified in B1P.

Section II

ᵉOr "that they may go down, the snakes of their holes."
All three mss. have n̰ instead of r̰ or m̰.

ᶠOr "canoe," smḥ.

ᵍCf. also PT 1654. Faulkner, Ancient Egyptian Pyramid Texts, p. 247, note 4, takes this as "protection," a reduplication of nḥ "protect."

ʰPerhaps "who binds" in B5C.

In CT 1136 the deceased by saying his own name expects the way to be opened that he may pass to this sealed place.

CT 1136 (6')

Cᵃ ⁴⁸¹Flame. Flame. ⌜The abode?⌝ ᵇ Sealed chamber of Mighty-face. I have come by the north winds.ᶜ ⟨Mine is⟩ᵈ the placeᵉ of Shu, with which Nun was full in the midst of ⌜Dendera⌝.ᶠ Mine is Authoritative-utterance who speaks in darkness, rich in hours. Open the way that I may pass to you thereby, by saying my name.ᵍ I have come here from Sepa.ʰ I have seen that which was in it. I am the one who saw and beheld.ⁱ I encountered the ⌜dom palm⌝.ʲ I have made Sepa secret. I have aided you as a youth.ᵏ ⁴⁸²What I said to you there is an enduring image. I am the one who carved the north winds of Sepa. I am the horizon which they ⌜experienced⌝.¹ My way is clean.

ᵃThis occurs in B1Be, B1P, and B5C.

ᵇỈꜥrw for Ỉꜥrt? Cf. Wb. I, 42, 6, for the 18th dynasty Ỉꜥrt meaning "Götterwohnung."

ᶜB1P has "I have come here by the wind."

ᵈThis is written ink instead of nnk as below, but "I am" seems less likely in this context.

ᵉBorghouts, Magical Texts, p. 94 note 162, suggests that the b with a stroke here is for "leg." Hans Goediche, The Report about the Dispute of a Man with his Ba, p. 73, note 138, suggests that it is for bꜣ.

ᶠApparently Bꜣwt, cf. Wb. I, 416, 14.

ᵍThese last two sentences were translated a little differently by Zandee, Death, p. 29.

ʰCf. Gardiner, Ancient Egyptian Onomastica, II, 127-128; cf. also ECT VI 213 k-1.

ⁱB1P adds "the form."

^j Written m% sp sn (?); also possible is m%h "sheaf."
^k Or "in name," m rn.
^l Written n dpt.sn, or is it an unknown verb ndp?

CT 1137 occurs at the middle of this group but lacks the double doors found in the other four. The deceased came from Babylon after he found a sealed box. He is "the one who protects the middle traps."

CT 1137 (7')

C^a   [482] Attacker.

I am the powerful one who robbed the Bowed-down one,^b the powerful one who is in darkness and who has not allowed that you be powerful over him among those who make every reproach and those who are in the neck of those who are from the protector who is in darkness.   ^483 I have come here from Babylon, after I found the sealed box^c which was stretched out in front of it.^d It is the one who goes down who testifies to me concerning the way^e on which I pass the spirit^f and those who are in the midst of Nun.^g I am the one who protects the middle traps.
⌜CROSS THE PLACE⌝.^h Mine is light.

^a This occurs in B1Be, B1P, and B5C.
^b Ksy, cf. Wb. V, 139, 4-5.
^c B1Be has "that the box was sealed."
^d Hr h(%)t.s (?), or "stretched out under the hts." B1Be has "and the hts (?) was stretched out."
^e Or continuing the preceding "by the one who went down after I testified concerning the way."
^f B5C seems to have "my spirit."
^g B1P has "the sky."
^h D% st, or enigmatic writing.

Section II

In spell 1138 the deceased opens darkness, passing more demons and flaming doors.

CT 1138 (8')

C^a [483]The sledge of Re. Flame. Flame.
I have come that I may be mighty together with you. It is this aggressor who reassembled Contrary-face ^{484}after Seth who made the dark eye passed by. I am the destroyer, (with) the lord of robbing accompanying me. I am the one who passes and who opens darkness. Flame is that which is not powerful over him as (over) another during the night. Mine is ⌜the tjerep-goose⌝.^{b} I have opened darkness.

^{a}This occurs in B1Be, B1P, and B5C.
^{b}Written with a $\underline{t}$ and the s$\underline{i}$-bird determinative. Cf. Wb. V, 337 and 387, 6-9.

CT 1139 ends the group similarly with additional interesting but incomplete references.

CT 1139 (9')

C^a [484]The one who is on the high walls.^{b} I die in its vicinity.^{c}
Flame. Flame.
The mouths^d of their snakes protect it. Reveal their^e names, (you) two comrades who are on his high wall.
^{485}Make a clean way for me, O lord of everlastingness who is in Maat.^{f} Broad^g is the way which does not embrace snakes. May darkness cease and light come to be. Mine is travelling. I have come here from this pure land, O Hapy. I found a plant there which was green. It was small but it grew. I recreated^h it when I breathed. It is I whom he placed in his vicinity. I am the one who cuts off the ⌜fetters⌝.^{i} Opener of Mouth^j in darkness. My nail. The one without his mother is Opener of Mouth. May I be mighty with my horn and your nail.

^aThis occurs in B1Be, B1P, and B5C.

^bOr "the one who is at the extreme ends."

^cM dr.s may be a play on imy drw. Again without an antecedent for s this could be m sdr "when I sleep."

^dB1P apparently has fnd "noses."

^eB1Be has s "its name."

^fB5C adds "his."

^gWsht, a feminine adjectival predicate ? An error? Or perhaps as Borghouts, Magical Texts, p. 63, note 88 "The breadth of the road is the tmm.t (hide?) of (the) snakes."

^hKmȝ, "(re)create" or "revive" from context. B5C has sn for kmȝ in error.

ⁱFor imy-ꜥ cf. also PT 1484d-e. Faulkner, Ancient Egyptian Pyramid Texts, p. 229, note 6, takes it as "in whom are hands" rather than "what is on the hands."

^jHbd-r, cf. Wb. III, 67, 9.

^kB1P has "Ba," B1Be has "father."

Spell 1140 is enclosed by a wall of black, "darkness." The bull that is pictured on B5C probably explains the use of "horn" and gives us an antecedent for "his" in "It is his horn which gives darkness, illness, and death." The bull could also have significance with regard to CT 1139 which concluded with "I am mighty with my horn and your nail." The deceased appeals to the gods (including Re, Atum, and Isis) for help against this demon.

CT 1140 (10')

C^a   486 He is in the midst of darkness. It is his horn which gives darkness, illness, and death. This is what is in that which is upon it at the great flaming doors. Opener of Mouth in darkness is his name. O Re, Atum, Nun, Old-one, and divine Isis, I have come here in fear. O Fiery-ones,^b I am the powerful one who went forth from the vultures in the daytime. My head is ⌜Rager⌝^c whose horns have been cut off in darkness. The slayer is your arm 487 according as it cuts off the head of the one who comes that he may oppose as god. It is I whom the goddess, the mistress, has borne. It is Imesty who purifies me when the hand^d of the destroyer of my power^e rages.^f

^{a}This occurs in B1Be, B1P, and B5C.

^{b}For htyw cf. Wb. III, 218, 14.

^{c}Hdn, cf. Wb. III, 214, 4-10, for New Kingdom words meaning "displeasure" or "rage" that may be related to this.

^{d}B5C has ht "belly."

^{e}Hm shm.i; since shm is without phonetic complements, perhaps the signs are in disorder again and hm should be omitted, "when the hand of my Power rages."

^{f}Or, "It is Imesty who cleans me by the raging of the hand of the destroyer of my power."

CT 1141 is for the most part surrounded by fire on B1Be. The deceased makes more claims and tells the demons to beware of him.

CT 1141 (11')

C^a [487]$_I$ am the one whom the^b fire illumines. I am the one who ⌈breaks⌉^{c} the^d ⌈fetters⌉, who shoots at underlings. O sailors,^{e} beware of me. I am the one who cuts off the middle rays^f (from) upon him. ^{488}I am the one who repels her, who gives her to the earth gods who are in the lake (and to) Geb, your protector. On your face! Do not examine his character.^{g}

^{a}This occurs in B1Be, B1P, and B5C.

^{b}B5C adds "his."

^{c}It is not clear how this word is to be read. I can only suggest an otherwise unknown šnpw "⌈break⌉" or a very unusual writing of šnt "fight."

^{d}B5C adds "his."

^{e}Nfw, or "Breezes."

^{f}⌈Stwt⌉ ?

^{g}Sp, or "misdeed."

In spell 1142 a demon is pictured on B5C and various gods are called upon for protection.

CT 1142 (12')

c^a [488] She whose name was presented in the midst of her fire. They, the ⌜Miserable-ones⌝,^{b} guard his house and her fire. Beware, O Earth-gods of the ⌜boat⌝.^{c} Stand! Protect! Re, Atum, Nun, Old-one, Shu, Iku, Nemu, and Hetep. ^{489}The woman has opposed the sick-one. They whose names were presented made her ⌜walls⌝.^{d} I am the one whom Re built, whom Shu built. Maat belongs to this god who is in the midst of flame, who has not placed the just-ones in himself^e With another command^f which went forth from his mouth on the day of protecting, his soul which you have commanded has protected me. He is driven off^g from these your ⌜wounds⌝^{h} while the underlings are worms^i upon you. I am Maat who is in the nail. If you come opposing me, then the Terrible-one will be expelled from the Earth-god and the Sharp-one from the Agressor, ^{490}until I retreat going and coming.

^{a}This occurs in B1Be, B1P, and B5C.

^{b}Possibly shwt for hswt "weak ones" or "miserable ones." Cf. also Wb. IV, 270, 9, shr, which Von Deines, WMT, p. 792, reads as sh.t "Krankheit" or "Krankheitsstoff."

^{c}Mdtn for m'ndt "day-bark"?

^{d}The translation of this sentence is little more than a wild guess. For "walls" I assume that snb somehow became nsp, otherwise "wounds."

^{e}Zandee, Death, p. 140, has offered a similar translation for this sentence.

^{f}Written m ky n hnwt.

^{g}Written htf for h(w).t(w).f?

^{h}Nsp here without a wall determinative.

^{i}Ddft in B1Be, but dft in B1P and B5C.

The enclosure of CT 1143 could be the garden mentioned in the spell. Numerous deities are invoked.

CT 1143 (13')

c^a [490] Repel the Terrible-ones from the Earth-gods!^{b} Protect the Great-one! Part the two warriors in six-hundred and three storms!

Section II

There are six-hundred in the breadth of this garden.[c] Shu, Nun, Atum, Re, the Old-one. I have passed Shu, Nun, Atum, Re, the Old-one, Seth,[d] Seth, Seth, Seth,[491] Ptah, Perception, He who is in his eye, He whose fire illumines his spirit, Terrible-one, Nun, She who has borne Body of Face,[e] who is more excellent than his brothers, Falcon, Bird, Feather on the day of scratching.[f]
They are safe after the destroying.[g] Their prayer[h] is everlastingness. ⌜Swim⌝[i] toward them,[j] O Secret-face. Make a picture of two arms at the time of your goings and comings, O Horus the elder, who is in the midst of the stars, the upper ones as well as the lower ones.

[a] This occurs in B1Be, B1P, and B5C.

[b] B5C has $\underline{d}$ for $\underline{dr}$. B1Be has "those who hinder the Earth-gods."

[c] Ḥry-š̃, cf. $\underline{Wb}$, III, 135, 11, for ḥryt-š̃ of 18th dynasty texts.

[d] Or sȝb "jackel," "dignitary."

[e] Ḥt-ḥr. B1Be has ḥr ḥt ḥr?

[f] Pȝḥ, cf. PT 440.

[g] B1P has "Feather on the day after the destroying."

[h] Nḥt. B1P and B5C have $\underline{r}$ instead of a bookroll determinative. B5C also has the tyw-bird instead of the nḥ-bird.

[i] What looks like bnš̃ is apparently for nbȝ "swim" or in B1Be "swimmer."

[j] B5C has "is the name of."

Spell 1144 probably includes two demons' names in a fiery enclosure.

CT 1144 (14')

C[a] [492] Sharp of anger.[b] Revealer[c]-guardian.

[a] This occurs in B1Be, B1P, and B5C.

[b] Zandee, $\underline{Death}$, pp. 24 and 246, uses "Painful of rage" for this name.

[c] Probably shȝy with misplaced ȝ. It could also be "⌜Protector⌝."

Spell 1145 has protecting deities within walls of fire. Of all the spells in this section, this provides perhaps the clearest and most complete description of what is taking place. The deceased is with Re on the solar bark, and he assists both by rowing and by forcing the gatekeepers to let them pass.

CT 1145 (15')

C[a] [492] The Protectors[b] whom he knows.[c] The warrior who guards him in the midst of his shrine. O Gray-haired one[d] who hears the sistrum player.
O PHYSICIANS, PROTECT ME EVERY DAY FROM THOSE WHOSE NAMES ARE UNKNOWN.[e] LORDS OF LIFE, BREATHE EVERY DAY ON THE ONE OPPOSED TO THEM.[f]
O you four gods whom the goddess, the mistress, bore,[g] the one who comes opposed to me is the destroyer,[h] and I cause him to know that I am the one who has borne you. O Unique One, I pass by [493] in order to satisfy the heart of the Trap-maker[i] that you may trap the shining day. The fingers in front of him (as well as) his hand are what blind. Rise up, O Heliopolitan of the desert.[j] I am the one who rows you again in accordance with your desire,[k] after he (Apopis) has shot at you. Your heart was taken[l] by Shu. I was excellent when I passed by[m] in your peace. Your power was divided by the Angry-of-mouth and your striking force was extinguished by[n] those who are in front of Shu and Authoritative Utterance, who raise an uproar in Nun. [494] I am the Powerful one, the aggressor.[o] This[p] is your shrine. I am your mighty one. Make way for me. I am a justified one who follows the Bloody-one.[q] I am a man of stature who will not be seen by those around him, who shoot ⌜arrows⌝.[r] Your voice was extinguished by those of Osiris. Swallow after you have chewed this muscle of your flesh which is in the midst of the Escaper.[s] If you come against me and if an arrow[t] comes passing by and stretching out behind me, [495] then Apopis under whom the hole coils will offer to him. I am the one who will speak.[u] Then Isis the Great whose house is under her[v] will offer to him. You are the one who speaks against me.

This great baboon who is among[w] the gods (will) offer to me, the one under him, with a crane and ⌜sutet⌝-bird.[x] May you fall[y] on your face. Depart! The god, the lord of the red[z] mansion which is in the horizon, comes[aa] peacefully. I am ⌜myself⌝.[ab] I pass your[ac] Trembler[ad] when Re shines peacefully.[ae]

[a] This spell occurs in B1Be, B1P, and B5C.
[b] Hꜣyw, cf. CDME, p. 161.
[c] Written ꜥmꜥ for ꜥm? Otherwise perhaps "engendered." For a substantive ꜥmꜥ cf. ECT V 24 d and PT 2206 a, which Speleers, Traduction, Index et Vocabulaire des Textes des Pyramides Égyptiennes, translated as "Male." For ꜥmꜥt meaning "Jungfrau" see Von Deines, WAD, p. 91; and see both ꜥmꜥ and ꜥmꜥt below ECT, VII 450 d.
[d] Skm in B5C is apparently nkm in B1P and B1Be, cf. Wb. II, 346, 6. B1P and B1Be add "in it," and B1P repeats "in the midst of his shrine, O Neken."
[e] A less likely translation for "FROM...UNKNOWN" would be "BY EXTINGUISHING THEIR NAMES."
[f] Or "WHO MAKE THE ONE OPPOSED TO THEM HAPPY." I propose reading snf m (or sndm) hsf r.sn for snf m.s rn hsf "EMPTY OUT OF IT THE OPPOSED NAME."
[g] Or "who have borne the goddess . . ."
[h] B5C has pn "this destroyer," B1Be and B1P have the sentence pronoun pw.
[i] Written irw (with reed-leaf, eye, mouth, and rw-lion)-hꜣdw.
[j] Or "red crown."
[k] This phrase occurs at the end of the sentence.
[l] B5C apparently has "was rowed."
[m] B1P and B1Be add "peacefully."
[n] B1P has n for in.
[o] Or "powerful of anger."
[p] Pꜣw could also be "Falsehood" or "Gossip."
[q] Or "Blood," snf.
[r] The meaning "arrows" is suggested by the determinative in B1P and B5C. Otherwise wnšw could be "jackals."
[s] Btktkw.
[t] Written šsrw. B1Be has "if you come against šsrw."
[u] B1Be has "I did not speak."
[v] Or "in her possession." Borghouts, Magical texts p. 58, note 62, suggests that this hr.f and another in ECT, VII 353c, are actually hrw.f and refer to the lower part of the body. I disagree especially in view of the parallel construction in 353c.

[w] B5C has "who eats."

[x] Otherwise unknown.

[y] Written ḥw in B5C with its fallen man determinative misplaced.

[z] Apparently the dšr-bird of B5C was corrupted to snd-goose in B1P, and this latter sign was spelled alphabetically in B1Be.

[aa] Cf. Polotsky, "Tenses," p. 20, with reference to this verb.

[ab] Written wỉ sp-2.

[ac] B1P omits k.

[ad] Nwrw is the name of a ferryman in PT 1183.

[ae] B5C has m ḥtp. B1P has m pt "in the sky," and B1Be is illegible.

Ct 1146 includes the plan of a building and has the label "Image of a mansion." The mansion has a demon gatekeeper and is the "place of a spirit." The deceased is very tall there but he cannot be seen in the dark. This is a goal of the deceased and the end of the preceding journey. It makes this section complete in itself as a guide to the beyond.

CT 1146 (16')

C[a] 496 Image of a mansion.[b]
He will sleep so that he may wake at the year's "Beginning of the Season" festival and so that his entourage may see him. It is the noise that is heard. It is the place of the demolisher who placed himself (in readiness) since he saw the perfect spirit.[c]
The way of passing him when he sails therein.
The sky, the earth and the horizon have been opened[d] to me, this N.
Place of a spirit. Place of excellent magic.
He is a man of countless (cubits) in his length. He is in the midst of darkness. He cannot be seen. This river is far from him. As for his entourage, it cannot be seen.
497 That which is in them and their mansions is the way of the goddess.
The Baboon, Countless, Authoritative Utterance, Demolisher, Hound, Protector, ⸢(the-one)-with-her⸣,[e] Heated-one and He-is-Firm.

As for the sky, the earth, and the horizon, that which is in them is the way of the goddess.

^aThis occurs in B1Be, B1P and B5C.
^bCf. Zandee, Death, p. 189 for his translation of parts of this spell.
^cB1Be has "who is placed since he saw the perfect spirit," and B5C has "who placed him, the perfect spirit, in his charge in his hand."
^dWritten wbꜣ in B5C but tbꜣ (?) in B1Be.
^eB1P has hnꜥ.s, but B1Be and B5C have ḥꜥs (?).

This whole section describes the journey of the deceased with the sun-god until the deceased reaches his goal at this mansion. Here we would expect to have some reference to Re but none occurs. We must assume rather that the deceased has reached Osiris as the introduction to this version suggests. It seems then that this original solar (Heliopolitan) tradition is being used in a work that is concerned principally with Osiris.

The spells of this second section might reasonably be expected to be comparable to those in section VIII (spells 1100-1110) of the longer group (versions A and B), since both have doors and keepers and apparently offset each other with regard to the central plan, but these two sections are neither similar nor unique in the Book of Two Ways as will be seen.

SECTION III

Spells 1036-1082 of versions A and B are paralleled more or less by the C-version spells, 1147-1185. CT 1036/1147 begins the map which includes sections III and IV. The map is divided horizontally into two compartments each having a zig-zag path, and the texts in the upper compartment make up section III while section IV consists of the texts in the lower compartment. The blue path or way in the upper compartment meets or almost meets the black lower way at the far end of the two compartments.

CT 1036 (7)

A[a]   ²⁸⁴I have come in the dignity of Shu.[b] I have treated Osiris. Make way for me.[c] ²⁸⁵⌜Clap⌝ your hand![d] That which is in my hand is the best[e] of the ⌜maces⌝[f] of Re. Depart![g]
IT IS[h] A SPELL FOR PASSING HIM.

B[i]   ²⁸⁴Being in[j] the sky of Osiris,[k] my thighs[l] having[m] the dignity of the head.[n] I am the one who has treated Osiris. ²⁸⁵Strike your forehead.[o] The one who is with me is ⌜He-of-the-maces⌝,[p] (also) ⌜He-of-the-lions⌝.[q] A spell for passing[r] him.

CT 1147 (17')

C[s]   ⁴⁹⁸The sky has been opened to Osiris who is before me when I am a mummy.[t] Clap your hand, O Re.[u] I[v] arise that ⌜Shu⌝[w] MAY PASS. I am the one who has treated Osiris.[x]

   [a]Version A occurs on B3C, B4C, B12C, B13C, B6C, B4L, B1Bo, B2Bo, and B4Bo. B9C has affinities to both versions A and B.
   [b]B12C has "my dignity being (that of) Shu," with m̲ of predication. B13C, B6C, and B4L omit m̲ and perhaps are to be read "I have come that I may ennoble Shu." B1Bo has "This N.

Section III

came after this N. had ennobled Shu." B9C and B4C have "in my dignity of Shu."

^{c}B12C, B13C, and B4L add "that I may pass."

^{d}Hw ꜥ.k, or, "Extend your arm."

^{e}Ḥꜣt, or "forepart."

^{f}Ḥdw, or "onions (?)."

^{g}B4L has srw tw, "remove yourself," for rw tw. B1Bo and B4Bo end here omitting the rubric.

^{h}B12C, B6C, B4L, and B2Bo omit pw as does B-version.

^{i}B-version mss. include B1L, B2L, B3L, B1C, and B2P.

^{j}B3L omits m, "As the sky belongs to Osiris, my thighs possess. . . ." B9C apparently substitutes n for m in error.

^{k}Cf. Zandee, Death, p. 26, for a different rendering.

^{l}B2P omits suffix. B1C has "my heir."

^{m}For this meaning of the preposition m cf. G. Lefebvre, Grammaire de L'Egyptien Classique, 2nd ed., 1955, §490, 8.

^{n}B2P omits n tp, and B3L omits the following statement.

^{o}Written ḥw n.k ḥꜣt.

^{p}Written hdw with a divine determinative. B9C has hdw Rꜥ. On B3L the spell ends here "Strike your forehead, you-of-the-maces"."

^{q}Rw(w), cf. also ECT I 2 b.

^{r}Written swꜣwꜣ in B1L, B2L, and B1C. B2P apparently has [s]wꜣt. B9C has r n swꜣhr.f pw as in version A.

^{s}Version C occurs in B1Be, B1P, B5C, and B4L.

^{t}Or, "Open the sky to Osiris (O you) who are before me as a dignitary."

^{u}B4L has "I am this Re."

^{v}Perhaps m-ꜥ.i is "with me," and a new sentence begins with "Arise."

^{w}Written šy with feather and divine determinative. B1P adds a chick-w.

The upper way of the map has Osiris, who is in the sky, as its central figure; but in this spell the emphasis on Osiris is clearer in versions B and C than it is in A. The protection or protectors with the deceased cannot be the object of the rubric nor would this be Osiris. The rubric probably refers to the spell below and its demon, the "Opposer-of-Demolishers." Only on B1C are most of the demons illustrated; the one accompanying spell 1037 is a ram-headed crocodile with human arm holding a knife. For passing him, a spell consisting of his name suffices as often below.

CT 1037 (8)

A[a] ²⁸⁶I have seen what I have treated in Osiris. Do not[b] mourn[c] over his[d] flesh.
The "Opposer-of-Demolishers."[e]

B[f] ²⁸⁶Flame.
I have seen what I have treated in Osiris. Do not mourn over his[g] flesh.
"Opposer-of-Demolisher" is his name.
²⁸⁷Gate of flame. GATE OF DARKNESS.

CT 1148 (18')

C[h] ⁴⁹⁸Flame.[i]
Make way for me that I may pass.[i] I treat Osiris. Do not mourn over his flesh.[j] Plough through[k] Shu with the knife. ⁴⁹⁹The "Opposer-of-Demolishers."
THE GATE OF DARKNESS IS ITS NAME. IT IS A SPELL FOR RECOGNIZING[l] THIS HIS NAME.[m]

[a] Version A occurs in B3C, B4C, B12C, B13C, B6C, B4L, B1Bo, B2Bo, B4Bo, and B9C. B6C has the label "Flame" like versions B and C.

[b] For this spelling of the negative imperative, cf. Edel, Alt. Gr., §1110.

[c] Kmꜣ in B4C and B1C, but generally kꜣw m or kꜣmw or even kꜣm m in B2L.

[d] B3C and B4C omit the suffix f.

[e] B13C and B4L also include the labels: "GATE OF DARKNESS. SPELL FOR THE LAKE OF [FLAME] WHOSE NAME IS ⌜THIS-ONE-IS-EFFECTIVE⌝," restoring nby for flame; for rn.f as logical subject preceding a name see Hornung, Amduat, I, p. 23 and often.

[f] Version B occurs in B1L, B2L, B1C, and B2P, with B3L having only the labels beginning with "Opposer."

[g] B1L omits f.

[h] Version C occurs in B1P, B1Be, B5C, and B4L.

[i] B4L omits sdt and swꜣ.i.

[j] B1P (in disorder here as de Buck noted) has "his flesh" immediately after "I" and the determinative of kmꜣ, "I ⌜his flesh⌝ which (fem.) I treat, Osiris."

[k] Cf. PT 1454a for hb as a verb. Cf. Borghouts, Magical texts, p. 84 note 133, for a different interpretation of this sentence.

Section III

¹Or "preparing" or unknown s&sjy&s;.

ᵐCompare B4L here to B4L in spell 1037 (note e above). Perhaps r n should be <u>rn</u> and this could be translated "The lake of [flame] is the name of this lake."

The separate compartment that contains this spell has a door at the top, usually painted red, and often labeled "flame," while in the lower part of the compartment there are two more labels designating places, a black semicircle called "Gate of Darkness" and another area called "Gate of Flame." It is an entrance or entrances to the ways beyond. Since the deceased had to know how to pass on both ways (CT 1035) and since the ways apparently meet at the far end of the map, we can assume that a circuit of the ways was intended beginning and ending at the gates of CT 1036. It will be seen that this circuit is associated with the voyage of solar and lunar barks through the sky (upper waterway) and underworld (land way.). Since spells 1058 and 1060 are concerned with the impending dawn, these should probably represent a point near the end of the journey through the underworld and we shall therefore proceed first from CT 1038 through 1054 in section III and then in reverse order from CT 1068/1069 to 1055 in section IV.

Spell 1038 gives the name of the first demon "keeper" beside the blue waterway. He appears in B1C as a human-headed crocodile with a knife in his hand. The text added to the name in B4Bo indicates clearly that the names of demons are to be known by the deceased if the deceased is to pass the demons.

CT 1038 (9)

A,Bᵃ [287]Miserableᵇ-of-Voice is its keeper.ᶜ

ᵃThis occurs in B3C, B4C, B12C, B13C, B4L, B2Bo, B4Bo, B9C, B1L, B2L, B3L, B1C, and B2P.

ᵇOr "Anxious," cf. Zandee, <u>Death</u>, p. 280.

ᶜB9C omits the predicate, <u>iry.s pw</u>. B4Bo adds "A spell for passing him is that which is beneath him."

Ct 1038 and 1039 do not occur in version C. An enclosure which indicates a mound, often painted yellow or white, has a list of several demons and this list is spell 1039. B3C and B4C have this mound and the other mounds below painted in regularly but without the spells (i.e., names).

CT 1039 (10)

A,B^a 288 Those who are in it:
   Leaper,^b Fierce-one, ⌜. . .⌝,^c Robber,^d Blasphemer, and ⌜. . .⌝.^e

^aThis occurs in B12C, B13C, B4L^{a,b}, B2Bo, B1L, B2L, B3L, B1C, and B2P. Some of these names also occur in BD 144.
^bWritten s3p, cf. Caminos, L.E.M., p. 187.
^cGenerally written ʿ3t, but also ʿ3tt in B13C and B4L and ʿ3mt in B2L.
^dT3, or "Male." B4L^b apparently has "Pellet." The last three names in B4L^a are "Confusion, Trembler, and Hot-One" as in spell 1041.
^eWritten ʿ3tîm but ʿ3tî in B3L.

In CT 1040/1150 the deceased is associated with the cities of Rosetaw and Pe, and apparently because of this he can serve as one of the guides either on the ways (C-version), on the horizon (B), or on the god's mounds (A). He would seem to be with the "entourage of flame" (CT 1128) helping to guide the solar bark past the entourage of Osiris, i.e., the demons.

CT 1040 (11)

A^a   289 I am one who was born in Rosetaw and Pe.^b Effectiveness was given to me by the^c lord, Re-Horakhte. My dignity is in Pe, 290 when^d I purify Osiris.^e I have received obeisance in Rosetaw while guiding the gods on their mounds.^f 291 I am one of their guides.

B^g   289 I am one who was born in glorious Rosetaw. Effectiveness was given to me by the lord of the Horizon.^h My dignity is in Pe 290 according as Osiris is pure.ⁱ I receive obeisance in Rosetaw and guide^j the gods on the horizon in the entourage around Osiris. 291 I am one of their guides.

Section III

CT 1150 (20')

C^k ^{500}I am one who was born in Rosetaw of the horizon. The horizon was given to me by the lord of the horizon. My dignity is in Pe according as Osiris is pure.^{i} Adoration is in Rosetaw while guiding the gods ⟨on⟩^{1} the ways in the entourage which is around Osiris. I am one of their guides.

^{a}Version A occurs in B3C, B4C, B12C, B13C, B4L, B1Bo, B2Bo, and B4Bo. B9C has affinities to both versions A and B. The text also occurs in BD 118 and 144c.
^{b}B13C, B4L, and B2Bo omit "Pe."
^{c}Suffix added: in B13C "my," in B4Bo "his."
^{d}M was written in all but B4Bo and B9C.
^{e}B9C adds sjk, "the dignitary."
^{f}B13C and B4L have "horizons" for "mounds."
^{g}Version B occurs in B1L, B2L, B1C, and B2P.
^{h}B9C has "lord, Re, of the horizon."
^{i}Or, "as a priest of Osiris."
^{j}B2L alone repeats the suffix.
^{k}Version C occurs in B1P, B1Be, B5C, and B4L.
^{1}Hr was omitted on all mss. but from the context and parallels "on" would be better than "of" here.

Spell 1041/1149 labels the demons who occupy another mound whose keeper appears as a bull-headed crocodile with a knife. In CT 1149 the waterway and mound have been stylized to look like a bark with a shrine. The demons in version C are called jhw, "spirits," and the keeper is expressly a door keeper. From this and the fact that the names of demons and whole spells from this section occur in Chapter 144 of the Book of the Dead where they are connected with the seven gates through which the solar bark passes, it seems that this section is not really unlike section II.

CT 1041 (12)

A^a [291]"Cursed-face" is its keeper.^{b}
Those who are in it:
"Hot-face," ^{292}"Loud-voice," "⌜Oppressor⌝,"^{c} "Confusion,"^{d}

"Trembler," and "Burner."ᵉ

B^f [291]."Cursed-face" is its keeper.
"Faceless,"ᵍ ²⁹²"Loud-voice," "⌜Equalizer⌝,"ʰ "Confuser,"
"Furious-one," "Burner," and ⌜. . .⌝.ⁱ

CT 1149 (19')

C^j [499] THE NAMES OF THE SPIRITS WHO GUARD THESE WAYS.
Those who are in it:
⌜. . .⌝,ᵏ "Seizer," "⌜Sheep⌝,"ˡ "Fierce,"ᵐ and "⌜. . .⌝."ⁿ
"Great-Face"ᵒ IS HIS NAME. HE IS THE KEEPER OF ITS DOOR.

CT 1152 (22')

C^p [501] ⟨Those who are in it:⟩^q
"Hot-face," "Loud-voice," "Oppressor," "Confusion,"
"Burner" is his name.

ᵃVersion A occurs in B3C, B12C, B13C, B2Bo, B4Bo, B9C, and B4L. Some of these names also occur in BD 144.

ᵇB3C stops here omitting the names which occur within the mound. B9C omits the predicate leaving only the name. B4Bo omits the rest of the spell and adds "A spell for passing him is that which is beneath him.

ᶜWritten ꜣy for ꜣry.

ᵈHꜣw, or "Monster," cf. Faulkner, Ancient Egyptian Pyramid Texts, § 226 note 2.

ᵉB4L has mnꜣm for šꜣm due to scribal error.

ᶠVersion B occurs in B1L, B2L, B3L, B1C, and B2P.

ᵍꞽn-ḥr, literally "Carried-off-of-face."

ʰOr perhaps "Mummy-wrapper," written my.

ⁱIllegible on all five coffins.

ʲVersion C occurs in B1P, B1Be, B5C, and B4L.

ᵏWritten ꜥtꜣhwt.

ˡWritten sꜣrtyw, cf. sr.t in Wb. III, 462, 14; cf. also ECT, VII 416 c.

ᵐWritten ꜣbs in all but B4L which has ꜣsb.

ⁿWritten pgpꜣ (?).

ᵒB4L has "Cursed-face" as in CT 1041. This is the only connection between these two spells.

^{p}Version C occurs in B4L, B1P, and B1Be. The names in B5C are illegible.

^{q}The three mss. are certainly incorrect here with $i̓ww$ or $i̓w\ m$ for $ntyw\ i̓m.s$.

In CT 1042/1151 the deceased identifies himself as a "spirit" and claims power over the other "spirits." He accompanies Re during the day and Thoth during the night along this waterway which represents the sky.

CT 1042 (13)

A^a ^{293}I am a spirit,^{b} the lord of spirits. The spirit which I have begotten,^{c} it exists; the spirit which I^d hate, it does not exist.^{e} ^{294}I am one who goes around his lake^f in flame, the lord^g of light. I make the circuit^h while the eye of Horus is beside me^i ^{295}As for Thoth, he crosses the sky^j in my presence.^{k} I pass safely.

B^l ^{293}I am a spirit, the lord of spirits. The spirit which I have begotten, it exists; the spirit which I hate, it does not exist.^{m} ^{294}I am the one who celebrates the monthly festival and announces the midmonth festival.^{n} I have made the circuit while the eye of Horus was beside Thoth at night,^{o} ^{295}as he crossed the sky, his seat being my seat. I pass safely.

CT 1151 (21')

C^p ^{501}I am a spirit, the lord of spirits.^{q} The spirits^r which I have begotten there, they exist; the spirit which I hate,^{s} it will not exist.^{t} I am one who celebrates the monthly festival, establishes the midmonth festival, and examines the eight. I am making the circuit because the eye of Horus is not beside the followers of Thoth.^{u} I have caused that it^v cross the sky that I may pass. I have not been afraid.

^{a}Version A occurs in B3C, B4C, B12C, B13C, B4L, B1Bo, B2Bo, and B4Bo. This text is also found in BD 144d.

ᵇPerhaps ꜣḫ should be left untranslated, cf. Žabkar, "Observations on T. G. Allen's Edition of the Book of the Dead," JNES, 24, pp. 85-86. I prefer however to use "spirit" for ꜣḫ to include both the deceased and demons. Allen's "blessed one" (BD, p. 232, note n) seems to be ruled out by the present context.

ᶜỊr, or possibly "have acquired," cf. Caminos LEM, p. 204, for ỉr as "get."

ᵈB3C also has the first person singular suffix here and occasionally elsewhere so this was undoubtedly the person of the text from which all the mss. were copied.

ᵉN ntf wn.

ᶠB13C has r for š in error.

ᵍB1Bo has nbt, "lady."

ʰB12C has "I have made the circuit."

ⁱB4L has "beside Thoth," and continues "when he crosses." The "eye of Horus" here and in ECT, VII 305 g-h, apparently designates either the moon or the lunar bark, but the term can also be used for the "solar bark" (CT 1071) and "offering" (CT 1123) in the Book of Two Ways just as in Pyramid Texts. B12C has a sun-disk instead of ỉrt "eye."

ʲB12C, B13C, and B4L have š, "lake," for pt.

ᵏFor₂ these last two sentences, B2Bo has "I have en[circled] ²⁹⁵ the sky [beside him]."

ˡVersion B occurs in B1L, B2L, B3L, B1C, B2P, and apparently B9C.

ᵐB1C has n ntf wn for n wnt.f.

ⁿThe reference to festivals found in versions B and C helps to show the intermediate position of version B between versions A and C.

ᵒWritten with an animal skin alone in B1L and B2L, cf. Clère and Vandier, TPPI, §15, 2,3, for this writing.

ᵖVersion C occurs in B1Be, B1P, B5C, and B4L.

ᵠB1Be has "I am the lord of the ⟨horizon⟩, a spirit."

ʳB4L omits the third ꜣḫ(w) which in B1Be is singular and in B1P is ꜣḫ.ỉ, "I am effective."

ˢB4L has tn for sfỉ, "Those that I have begotten, they exist there; the one which I distinguish...."

ᵗN wnn.f is omitted on B1Be, but occurs in all other mss.

ᵘ"Thoth" is partially restored on B4L and lost on the other mss.

ᵛWritten only in B4L.

Spell 1044/1154 is another list of names in a mound.

Section III

CT 1044 (15)

B[a] [296] "Fierce-one,"[b] "Watchful-of-heart," "Watchful-of-face,"[c] "Alert-one," "Sharp-one,"[d] and "Investigator."[e]

CT 1154 (24')

C[f] [502] "Mixer,"[g] "Watchful-of-heart," "Alert-one," "Noisy," ⌜. . .⌝.[h]

[a] These names occur in B2Bo, B1C, B1L, B2L, B3L, and B2P. Some of the names also occur in BD 144.
[b] Written $j\check{s}bw$, for $jsbw$ (?).
[c] B1L omits this name.
[d] Spd, or "Skilled-one." B2Bo has hrw, "Noisy-one," as in version C.
[e] $Smtw$, cf. Caminos, LEM, p. 178; or "Tormentor," cf. von Deines, WMT, II, 754.
[f] These names occur in B1Be, B1P, B5C, and B4L.
[g] Written $\check{s}b$, or should it be $j\check{s}b$ as in A and B. B4L has the $\underline{3}$-vulture after the flame determinative.
[h] ⌜Db^c⌝ rw (?).

Spell 1043/1155 accompanies a demon who in version A is keeper of a byway which the deceased is told to avoid. Only B3C, B2P, and B4L illustrate a byway on their plans that can be related to that of the text. Version B has the name of a demon, and the name is the spell for passing it. Two (A and C) or three (B) demons are named in CT 1045/1156; two are depicted on B1C. The "way" mentioned only in version B is not clearly depicted there but it can have several possible referents on plans of A-version coffins. It might be the stylized serpent of B1C, the waterway itself coming to a sharp point, or the dead end seen on B4C, the waterway itself coming to a sharp point, or the dead end seen on B4C. The one way mentioned in CT 1156 seems to cover the two byways shown clearly on all C-version coffins and treated separately in the longer group (CT 1043 and 1045).

CT 1043 (14)

A[a] [295]"Adorned-of-face"[b] is its[c] keeper. [296]This is its way.[d] You should not pass on it.

B[e] [295]"Tortoise." [296]A spell for passing him.

CT 1045 (16)

A[f] [297]"Flesh-of-the-enemy." "He who lives in[g] ⌜Fledgling-lake⌝",[h] "Furious-of-fire."[i] "He-whose-face-⌜glows⌝[j]-with-beauty."

B[k] [297]"He-who-lives-on-silence" is its name. "Furious-of-fire" is its name. "⌜Glowing⌝" is its name.[l] This is the way which is known[m] for reversion-offerings.[n]

CT 1155 (25')

C[o] [503]"Turtoise," adorned of face, in order to pass it.[p]

CT 1156 (26')

C[q] [503]This is its[r] way which is in the temple. You should not go on it. "MY-FLESH-IS-AFLAME." He should not turn back on it. "Aggressor" IS ITS NAME. HE WILL CHARGE DOWN UPON[s] ITS STRIKING-FORCE. "Furious-of-fire" is its name.

[a] Version A occurs in B3C, B12C, B13C, B4L. B2Bo, and B4Bo. B1C has affinities to both versions A and B.

[b] S̱tw-ḥr, or "⌜Equipped⌝-of-face," cf. Faulkner, CDME, p. 273.

[c] S is omitted on B2Bo and B4Bo.

[d] After this B1C concludes with "This is a spell for passing it."

[e] Version B occurs in B1L, B2L[a,b], B3L, and B9C.

[f] Version A occurs in B3C, B4C, B2Bo, B4Bo, and B1C.

[g] B2Bo and B4Bo add gs "at the side of," and B1C has m gs-pr, "in the district of. . ."

[h] Tȝ-š (?). B2Bo and B1C add "is its name," and omit the other names.

[i] Cf. PT 397 for nhd which Speleers translated as "furieux" and which Faulkner translates as "conquer." For nhdhd meaning "throb" cf. CDME, p. 136.

Section III

ʲB4Bo omits nhd ns hr and begins again with ẖmdw (?) for ẖdmw (?). This word is also written dỉmm and ẖdmm, and "glow" is merely a guess at its meaning.

ᵏVersion B occurs in B1L, B2L, B3L, and B9C. B2L and B9C begin with "Flesh-of-the-enemy."

ˡB9C omits rn.f pw after all of these names.

ᵐB2L and possibly B3L could have "which I know."

ⁿrd-wdbw for wdb-rd; or "which is known on the stairway of Djebu," B2L has rwdw and B9C and B1L could be rdw. For Dbw cf. Wb. V, 553, 2; and Hornung, Amduat, no. 195.

ᵒVersion C occurs in B1Be, B1P, B5C, and B4L.

ᵖPerhaps this should be "A spell for passing it" as in version B. B1Be omits r, "Pass it!"

ᑫVersion C occurs in B1Be, B1P, B5C, and B4L.

ʳB1Be, omits s "the way."

ˢHỉ, or "TACKLE."

Spell 1046/1158 accompanies another mound whose occupants are called followers of Osiris. This mound has its own master and seems to be a place of rest for those who have been protecting on the way.

CT 1046 (17)

Aᵃ ²⁹⁸He who gives effectiveness, the lord of reversion-offeringsᵇ (is) in it among the followers of Osiris.ᶜ The followers who are in it areᵈ the spirits which sit in itᵉ ²⁹⁹after they have protected their lords there.

Bᶠ ²⁹⁸He who gives effectiveness, the lord of reversion-offeringsᵍ is in it among the followers of Osiris. The followers are in itʰ ²⁹⁹when they have protectedⁱ their lords.

CT 1158 (28')

Cʲ [504] HE WHO GIVES EFFECTIVENESS, JUSTIFICATION,ᵏ AND REVERSION-OFFERINGS IN IT AMONGˡ THE GODS. IT IS OSIRIS WHO IS IN IT, AND THE SPIRITᵐ WHICH SAT IN IT AFTER THEY REACHED THEIR LORDS.

[a]Version A occurs in B3C, B4C, B12C, B2Bo, B4Bo, B1C, and B4L.

[b]B4L writes ꜥnd, "dawn," for (w)dbw.

[c]B4L has "of Re and Osiris."

[d]While the previous statement lacked the particle iw in a sentence with adverbial predicate, this statement has iw very exceptionally before a sentence with nominal predicate.

[e]B12C has im.sn, "with them."

[f]Version B occurs in B1L, B2L, and B3L.

[g]Or unknown dbw.

[h]Either mm for m, or perhaps s should be emended to sn, "among them."

[i]B1L has stp.sn sꜣ.sn n while most other mss. have stp.sn sꜣ r.

[j]Version C occurs in B1P, B1Be, B5C, and B4L.

[k]Written mꜣꜥ in all but B1Be which has mꜣꜥ hrw.

[l]B1Be has m for mm.

[m]Plural in B5C.

Spells 1047 and 1048 should be the same spell, but the two versions (A and B) were presented as separate spells in the de Buck edition because they differ significantly here. The deceased serves Osiris by cooking for him among those who make offerings. In versions B and C the deceased is said to have plots of land in the Field of Offerings and to be a scribe of the lands beside Thoth.

CT 1047 (18)

A[a] [299] That which Anubis bewails[b] is the day's offerings of straw[c] among[d] those who prepare ⸢fragrant-food⸣[e] for Osiris. I am the one who is beside[f] Thoth. 300 I am the one who cooks[g] the ⸢fragrant-food⸣ for Osiris among those who make offerings. That which Anubis bewails is the day's offerings of straw.[h]

CT 1048 (19)

B[i] [300] I am a pure one who cooks for Osiris daily. My plots of land are (in) the Field of Offerings, among the wise, 301 among those who prepare ⸢fragrant-food⸣[j] for Osiris.[k]

Section III   53

I am the scribe of the plots of land beside Thoth. I am the attendant[1] of Osiris among those who make offerings. That which Anubis bewails is offerings. (They) cannot be taken from me.[m]

CT 1159 (29')

C[n] 505(My) two plots of land are (in) the Field of Ḥetep among those who know, so that I may take care of Osiris there.[o] I am the scribe of the plots of land[p] beside Thoth. I am a pure one who cooks for Osiris daily among those who know offerings.

CT 1161 (31')

C[n] 506My two plots of land are (in) Ḥetep.[q] (They) cannot be taken from me.

[a]Version A occurs in B3C, B4C, B12C, B13C, B2Bo, B4Bo, and B4L. The text also occurs in BD 144f.

[b]B12C seems to have "the joy of Anubis is there and the offerings of straw are among . . ." It has ḥꜥwt for ḥꜣt, but the reed-leaf of im seems to have been misplaced from Inpw.

[c]Or "the offerings on the day of straw," cf. Allen, BD, p. 232, note x. Rw is apparently an earlier example of the word referred to in Wb, II, 408, 2; and WMT, I, 525.

[d]Or "from," cf. mm for m in CT 1034, note m.

[e]Following Allen, but cf. Wb, III, 294, 10, "verdorbenes"; and WAD, p. 399 for hnmt.

[f]iry-ꜥ.

[g]B13C has the "lasso"-sign instead of the "brazier"-determinative and B12C has the phonetic complement and determinative added to wꜣ, giving ink pf swꜣ, "I am that one who passes."

[h]B3C omits m ḥtpw and so has "That which Anubis bewails on the day of straw."

[i]Version B occurs in B1L, B2L, B3L, and B1C.

[j]B1C has hnmt. On B2P one group is lost and htm is left. B1L had htm alone. B2L has ht, "offerings."

[k]The spell ends here on B2P.

[l]Hnmt.

[m]N itw m-ꜥ.i, or "There is none who can take (them) from me."

[n]Version C occurs in B1Be, B1P, B5C, and B4L.

[o] B1Be omits "there." Cf. Zandee, Death, p. 4, for his translation of this spell.

[p] B1P and B5C add "of Ḥetep." B4L has "of Osiris and Ḥetep."

[q] Or, "in peace." B1Be has "offerings."

CT 1049/1160 identifies an enclosed area as the "Field of Offerings," the well known Elysian Fields or Paradise of the ancient Egyptians. Surprisingly, all but one of the coffins with version A omit the identifying texts here. Version A of B4L has the list of names from CT 1039 in place of this spell.

CT 1049 (20)

A[a] [301] A basket[b] of offerings, in which[c] (there is) ⌜fragrant-food⌝ for its lord, 302 from which ⌜fragrant-food⌝ goes forth to Osiris every day.

B[d] [301] The Field of the Eye[e] of the lord, in which (there is) an attendant for Osiris with offerings in the Field of Offerings. 302 Its lord has gone forth having prepared ⌜fragrant-food⌝ in it for Osiris every day. Offerings.

CT 1160 (30')

C[f] [505] The Field of making[g] offerings in which (there is) an attendant for Osiris, and from[h] which the Field of Offerings goes forth to Osiris daily.

[a] This occurs on B2Bo alone.
[b] Nbtt (?)
[c] Sn the suffix pronoun here is plural but nbtt was singular and the resumptive in ECT, VII 302 b, is also singular.
[d] Version B occurs in B1L, B2L, B2P, and B1C.
[e] B1C has "The Field of Ḥetep in which there is (wnn for wnnt) an attendant for Osiris, who is in the Field of Ḥetep, its lord, (an attendant) who eats offerings in it with Osiris every day. 302 Offerings."
[f] Version C occurs in B1Be, B1P, B5C, and B4L.
[g] B1Be omits irt, "The Field of Offerings."

^{h}B1 Be has $\underline{iw}$ for $\underline{im}$ in error.

The rubric in CT 1164 clearly designates the "Field of Hetep/Offerings" as a goal of the deceased. The deceased who reaches this goal cannot die or be opposed and he will see Osiris and Thoth every day.

CT 1051 (22)

A^a 303 ⟨Being with⟩^{b} the offerings which are in the suite of Osiris every day, (the suite) which eats bread among the living forever. The one whose plots of land will be there ^{304}will be with Thoth. He cannot be opposed by any Evil-one.

CT 1050 (21)

A^a [302]Spell for being a god (repeat)^c for Osiris. The one who sees Osiris cannot suffer death. The keeper of the gate is one who carries off by robbery.

CT 1051 (22)

B^d ^{303}SPELL FOR BEING WITH THE OFFERINGS AMONG THE GODS WHO ARE IN THE SUITE OF OSIRIS EVERY DAY. THEY EAT BREAD AMONG THE LIVING AND THEY^e CANNOT DIE FOREVER.
THE ONE WHOSE PLOTS OF LAND WILL BE THERE ^{304}WILL SEE OSIRIS EVERY DAY WITH THOTH. HE CANNOT BE OPPOSED BY THE EVIL-ONES, THE LORDS OF THE GATES, WHO CARRY OFF BY ROBBERY.

CT 1162 (32')

C^f [506]SPELL FOR BEING IN THE FIELD OF HETEP EVERY DAY AMONG THE FOLLOWERS OF OSIRIS, AND AMONG THE FOLLOWERS OF THOTH WHO EAT BREAD AMONG THE LIVING, WHO CANNOT DIE,^{g} AND IN WHOSE NOSES THERE IS BREATH.^{h}

CT 1164 (34')

C^f [507]IT IS THE PLACE OF A SPIRIT WHO CANNOT DIE FOREVER.
As for any person whose^i plots of land will be in the Field

56   *The Ancient Egyptian Book of Two Ways*

of Hetep, he will see^j Osiris every day with Thoth, and he cannot be opposed by the Evil-ones, the keepers^k of the gates among those who send robbers.

^a Version A occurs in B3C, B12C, B13C, B2Bo, B4Bo, and B4L.

^b Written nn m in all six A-version mss.; probably a corruption of wnn m with loss of the hare, but perhaps the scribes took this as "These are."

^c Or perhaps "local god," as B12C and B13C seem to have. B2Bo possibly has "(of) Re and Osiris."

^d Version B occurs in B1L, B2L, B2P, and B1C.

^e B1L omits sn.

^f Version C occurs in B1Be, B1P, B5C, and B4L.

^g B4L adds "forever."

^h B5C does not have this last clause rubricized.

^i B4L omits f.

^j Cf. Polotsky, "Tenses," p. 20.

^k B4L omits iryw, "The Evil-ones of the gates."

Spell 1052 names places that have plants, fields, sand and stone at the end of the waterway. Perhaps the places indicated here should be related to places in the lower half of the vignette from BD 110.

The heading of spell 1052 in version B is paralleled by 1180 in version C, and this heading really marks the beginning of section V (for ECT, VII 304 e, see below). On some source this part of the text was written in the wrong compartment.

CT 1052 (23)

A,B^a [304] The place of plants.^b The place of plots of land. The place of sand. The place of ⟨stone⟩.^c
The house of ⌈the protectress⌉.^d It is the spell^e which is over the (four) lakes.^f

CT 1163 (33')

C^g   507 ⌈Protectress⌉^h is its name. As for that one who is its master, it is Shu.^i

Section III

^aVersion A occurs in B2Bo and version B occurs in B1L and B2L.
^bSm.
^cỉnš for ỉnr?
^dOr is this ỉht-wtt? Cf. Wb, I, 125, 10. B1L and B2L have ỉhwtit and B2Bo has ỉhwyt.
^eB2L has š, "lake."
^fB2Bo has "The house of ⌜the protectress⌝ is this its name. The [pla]ce of sa[nd]. The place of [sto]ne. . . ."
^gVersion C occurs in B1Be, B1P, B5C, and B4L.
^hỉhyt.
ⁱšy, cf. ECT, VII 498 d.

It is clear that the description of "life" in the "Field of Offerings" from CT 1047-1052 is not quite the paradise or Elysian Fields which we have come to know from BD 110 (which also occurs in CT 464-468). The picture in version A is haphazard, but in B the deceased appears as no more than a servant who works all day for Osiris. The "Field of (the god) Ḥetep" or the "Field of Offerings" is placed here along the waterway, but the path is not necessarily directed to the enclosure and actually goes beyond on all coffins. The deceased can evidently work here all day as well as guide the barks.

CT 1053 which has its parallel in 1153, 1157 and 1165, occurs mainly on coffins with versions B and C, and is a spell to enable the deceased to cross to his goal by identifying himself with the moon.

CT 1053 (24)

A^a   305This is the way to the cities of those living on ⌜sweets⌝.^b This which is before is a spell for passing on it, a spell for passing the cities of ⌜those-of-the-knives⌝^c and those-loud-of-voice,^d and a spell for passing the way of those-of-flame.^e
I am the eye of Horus, excellent in the night, which makes flame with its beauty.   306I am lord of the horizon, the flame of every day licks^f me. [If I] pass [on the way] in its presence, [Apo]pis (will) really (be) opposed.
Spell ⟨for⟩^g reaching those^h squatters,ⁱ the keepers of the gates.

B[j] ³⁰⁵Those living on the ⌜sweets⌝ of Osiris there. This which is before is a spell for passing it, a spell for passing[k] the cities on the ways of ⌜those-of-the-knives⌝ who are loud-of-voice. This is its way downward. May you not pass on it. A spell for passing the way[l] of those-of-flame. I am the eye of Horus, that eye variegated by the flame of its[m] beauty. ³⁰⁶I am lord of the horizon. When Khepri shines, he licks me. If I pass, Apopis[n] will really be overthrown.
It is a spell for reaching the eldest (of) the six gate-keepers.

CT 1153 (23')

C° ⁵⁰²This is the way to the city of those living on their ⌜sweets⌝. THIS WHICH IS BEFORE IS A SPELL FOR PASSING IT. IT IS A SPELL FOR PASSING THE SHARP-ONES.[p] I AM THE ⌜PROTECTOR⌝.[q] THE LOUD-OF-VOICE[r] ARE THOSE WHO ARE ⌜ABOVE⌝.[s]

CT 1157 (27')

C° ⁵⁰⁴Spell for passing the way[t] of flame. I am that eye of Horus[u] which is excellent at night, the eye[v] of flame in its beauty.

CT 1165 (35')

C° ⁵⁰⁸As for (anyone) who passes the bend of this lake, he falls. There is no opposing that man. THEN THE MAN SAYS, [De]part, [squatters], keepers of the gates.

[a]Version A is represented only by B2Bo but it is quite different from the B-version.
[b]Written bn(i̯)t, cf. Wolfgang Schenkel, "Die Wurzel bnj 'süss'," MDAIK, 20 (1965), 115.
[c]Dsw.
[d][Kh]3-hrw, cf. CDME, p. 286.
[e]Sdtyw.
[f]Emending nsbw to nsb ⟨.s⟩.

Section III   59

^{g}B2Bo omits <u>n</u> which is found in the B-version mss.
^{h}<u>Ỉpw</u>.
^{i}<u>Mỉsw</u>, cf. P. Barguet, "Le Livre des Deux Chemins," Revue d'Égyptologie, 21 (1969) 9.
^{j}Version B occurs in B1L, B2L, B3L, B2P, and B1C.
^{k}B1C repeats " {it} ."
^{l}Plural in B1C.
^{m}B1L omits <u>s</u>.
^{n}B1C has "the enemies [and] Apopis."
^{o}Version C occurs in B1P, B1Be, B5C, and B4L.
^{p}<u>Mdsw</u>.
^{q}<u>Nḥ</u>.
^{r}<u>Ḥ3w-ḥrw</u>.
^{s}Or, "THIS IS A SPELL FOR PASSING THE SHARP ONES AND THESE LOUD-OF-VOICE WHO ARE ABOVE (or, WHO ARE AT THE GATE)."
^{t}B4L has "city." B5C and B1Be are illegible.
^{u}B1P apparently omits <u>Ḥr</u> after <u>nt</u>.
^{v}Perhaps this <u>irt</u> should not have had a stroke after it, "which makes flame." Roccati, Papiro Ieratico, p. 28 note a, has also taken <u>irt</u> this way.

Spell 1054/1166 identifies the flaming lake which separates the two ways and which cannot be crossed.

CT 1054 (25)

A,B^a [306]The lake of flame,^{b} ⌈Aatiu⌉ ^{c} is its name. There is no one who knows how to enter into the flame from which he is turned back.^{d} "He inherits the way" is the name^e of the true lake.

CT 1166 (36')

C^f [508]This is the lake of flame, ⌈Aatiu⌉ ^{g} is its name. There is no one who falls into the flame from which he is turned back.^{h} O you four Nemu,^{i} the real lake is "fish are the heirs."^{j}

^{a}Version B occurs in B1L, B1C, B2L, and B3L. The text of B2Bo is largely lost now but was probably similar. The A-version in B13C and B4L consists of only š̌ and š̌, š̌ respectively.

[b] B2L has "Spell for the lake of flame."

[c] ꜥꜣtyw.

[d] Similarly translated by Schott, "Zum Weltbild der Jenseitsführer des neuen Reiches," (<u>Nachrichten</u>), Göttingen, 1965, p. 192.

[e] B2Bo omits <u>rn</u>. B1C and B2L have <u>r n</u>, "spell for," instead of <u>rn</u>, "name."

[f] Version C occurs in B₁P, B1Be, B5C, and B4L.

[g] Again ꜥꜣtyw, but B4L has ꜥntyw.

[h] Cf. Zandee, <u>Death</u>, pp. 139-40, for his translation of this much of the spell.

[i] Cf. <u>ECT</u>, VII 488 n, and <u>PT</u>, 434e.

[j] B4L has "Its real name is 'Its fish are the heirs.'"

SECTION IV

On most coffins the texts of sections III and IV occur within the plan that was drawn. I have shown that the two mss. that lack the plan were also copied from sources that had the plan, and there are obvious errors in their arrangement of the texts (cf. JAOS, 91, 35-6). Thus we can judge for ourselves what the order of these texts is supposed to be, and based on the contents of the spells I propose taking the texts in reverse order from that of B4Bo which de Buck followed. Spells 1068 (A) and 1069/1179 (B and C) then are each first in this section for their respective versions.

CT 1068 (39)

A[a]   329Hail to you, O Re. May you propitiate the face of Osiris[b] for me that those who are in the netherworld (ỉmht) may worship you, 330that those who are in the underworld (dwȝt) may glorify you, and that they may give adoration to you when you come[c] in peace. May you give offerings to the great ones, abundance to the little ones. 331May you give offerings to me that I may attain the revered state like Re every day.

[a]The text occurs in B3C, B12C, B13C, B1Bo, B2Bo, B4Bo, B4L, and B9C.
[b]B3C has "May you propitiate Osiris."
[c]Cf. Polotsky, "Tenses," p. 5, for the circumstantial sdm.f, here written ỉwy, ỉy, and ỉw.

The deceased beseeches Re to permit him to attain Re's revered state. It is possible that this spell was intended to tie together the water and land ways. The two place names need not be identical here but could actually designate the two parts of the map. Ỉmht may be the sky or the part of the sky in which Osiris has his abode, and through which Re passes in the day. Dwȝt may be the underworld through which Re passes at night. CT 1068 is significant for giving dominence to Re not only on the land way but on the whole map. The emphasis on Re in the long versions and on Osiris in the short version becomes more evident as we proceed.

The first spell in version B is really the second half of CT 1069 which is paralleled by 1179. In this spell the deceased seems to be identified with Seth. In CT 1118-1119 Seth has his place in the sky beside Osiris and in 1128 he is found on the sun bark.

CT 1069 (40)

B[a] [332] I am the ⌜noise-maker⌝[b] of the sky who presents Maat to Re, who repels the strength of Apopis, who opens the firmament, who opposes the storm, and who nourishes the crew of Re. 333 My ⌜špt-cloth⌝[c] and my rod have been given to me. I have caused Ḥetep[d] to go up as its[e] keeper.[f] I have caused the bark to make good progress.[g] Make way for me that I may pass.[h]

CT 1179 (49')

C[i] 517 I am "Numerous-of-faces," who makes thunder,[j] whom Re raised up, who repels the strength of Apopis, who opens the firmament, who opposes the storm of those whom Re has nourished. My ⌜špt-cloth⌝ and my rod have been given to me. I magnified Ḥetep as its keeper and caused for myself that the bark make good progress. Make my way for me.[k] It is the one who guards him in the midst of his shrine. THIS WHICH IS BEFORE HIM IS A SPELL FOR PASSING IT.

[a] Version B occurs in B1L, B2L, B3L, B1C, and B2P. Cf. also BD 144.
[b] Written ꜥšꜣ ỉr hrw, but C-version has ꜥšꜣ hrw ỉr hrw, certainly easier to handle, and BD has the shorter ꜥšꜣ hrw, "garrulous."
[c] Cf. H. Fischer, "Varia Aegyptiaca," JARCE, II (1963) 25.
[d] B2L has "offerings."
[e] B1L omits the suffix f.
[f] Or, "Companion." B3L has "keeper" as feminine.
[g] ỉr šmt nfrt, literally, "make good movement."

Section IV

^{h}B1L adds the particle r.į.
^{i}Version C occurs in B1Be, B1P, B5C, and B4L.
^{j}Hrw pt, "the noise of the sky." For Seth as the thunder-god, cf. Papyrus Chester Beatty I, recto xvi, 4, in A. Gardiner, The Library of A. Chester Beatty, Oxford, 1931. Cf. also H. Te Velde, Seth, God of Confusion, Leiden, 1967, pp. 99-108.
^{k}B4L has "Make ⟨way⟩ for me that I may pass."

The first half of spell 1069 has its parallel in the first part of 1176 plus 1178. Two more demon-keepers are presented.

CT 1069 (40)

B^a [331]"Great-face," who opposes the aggressors and who guards them^b in its house. This is the one who enters under the bend. O Serket, I shall exist in the length of eternity. ^{332}THIS IS THE KEEPER OF THE BEND. "⌜Evil-of-mace⌝,"^{c} whose mother is called "Majestic-cat."^{d} THIS IS THE KEEPER OF THE BEND. THIS IS THE GUARDIAN IN THE MIDST OF ITS SHRINE. A SPELL FOR PASSING IT IS THIS WHICH IS BEFORE IT.

CT 1176 (46')

C^e [515]This is the one who enters under the bend of the lake. O Serket, I shall exist in the length of eternity.

CT 1178 (48')

C^e [516]THIS IS THE KEEPER OF THE BEND OF THE LAKE. "Great-face," who opposes the aggressors.
THIS^f IS THE KEEPER OF THE BEND OF THE LAKE. "Mild-of-form,"^{g} whose mother is called "Majestic-cat." The one who guards them (those that I placed against her) in its house.

^{a}Version B occurs in B1L, B2L, B3L, B1C, and B2P. Cf. also BD 144.
^{b}St.
^{c}Nfȝ-hd. B2L has hnfȝ-irw, "⌜pretentious⌝-of-form."
^{d}Miw-šft.

ᵉVersion C occurs in B1Be, B1P, B5C, and B4L.
ᶠB1Be, B5C, and B4L have only one pw.
ᵍB4L has nfꜣ, "Evil-one."

A ram-headed keeper of a bend is named in CT 1066/1177.

CT 1066 (37)

Aᵃ ³²⁷Its name is "Opposedᵇ-face," with face in ⌜dung⌝."ᶜ
This is the keeper of the bend.ᵈ It is a spell for passing it.ᵉ

Bᶠ ³²⁷Its name is "Opposed-face," living on ⌜dung⌝. This is the keeper of the bend. This is a spell for passing it.

CT 1177 (47')

Cᵍ ⁵¹⁶"Opposed-face," with face in ⌜dung⌝. THIS IS THE KEEPER OF THE BEND OF THE LAKE. THIS THAT IS ON IT IS A SPELL FOR PASSING IT.

ᵃVersion A occurs in B3C, B12C, B13C, B2Bo, B4Bo, and B4L.
ᵇOr, "repulsive," cf. Allen, BD, p. 230.
ᶜWritten jrwt for jꜣrwt? cf. Von Deines, WMT, p. 19, "Ausfluss."
ᵈB12C, B13C, B2Bo, and B4L omit this statement.
ᵉB4Bo and B9C omit this statement.
ᶠVersion B occurs in B1L, B2L, B9C, and B1C.
ᵍVersion C occurs in B1Be, B1P, B5C, and B4L.

CT 1067/1176 (second part) presents the deceased as a messenger and interpreter for Re.

CT 1067 (38)

A,Bᵃ ³²⁸I am the one who conducts the sacred writings to the god, Re.ᵇ I have come that I may ⌜explain⌝ᶜ the message to its lord.

Section IV

CT 1176 (46')

$^{C^d}$ [515f]$_I$ am the one who conducts the sacred writings to Re. I have come that I may ⌜explain⌝ the message to its lord.

^{a}The text occurs in B3C, B12C, B13C, B1Bo, B2Bo, B4L, B4Bo, B9C, B1C, B1L, B2L, and B3L. Cf. BD 136e.

^{b}B12C omits "Re." B1Bo has "Atum." The B-version represented by B1L, B2L, B3L, B1C, and B9C has "to the gods and Re."

^{c}Cf. Allen, BD, p. 222, note ac, for this meaning of sdb; or "⌜penetrate⌝...of its lord."

^{d}Version C occurs in B1Be, B1P, B5C, and B4L.

Spell 1065 has no parallel in version C. It has a later parallel in part of BD 130 while the other spells in this section are paralleled by BD 144. The other much longer part of BD 130 is represented by CT 1099 which likewise does not occur in version C. Together CT 1065 and 1099 describe the voyage of the sun-bark by day and by night.

CT 1065 (36)

A^a ^{324}Open, sky; open, earth. Open, eastern^b horizon; open, western horizon. Open, shrine of Upper Egypt; open, shrine of Lower Egypt. Open, doors.^{c} ^{325}Open,^{d} eastern doors to Re that he may go forth from the horizon. Open to him,^{e} double leaves of the night bark; open^c to him, doors of the day bark^f that he may inhale Shu, ^{326}that he may create Tefnut, that those who are in the suite may follow him, and that they may follow me like Re every day.

B^g ^{324}Open, sky; open, earth. Open, east; open, west. Open, shrine of Upper Egypt; open, shrine of Lower Egypt. Open, doors. ^{325}Open,^{d} doors, to Re that he may go forth from the horizon. Open to him, double leaves of the night bark; open^d to him, doors of the day bark,^{h} that he may inhale Shu, ^{326}that he may create Tefnut, and that those who are in ⌜this⌝^{i} suite may follow him like Re every day.

^{a}Version A occurs in B3C, B12C, B13C, B1Bo, B2Bo, B4Bo, B4L, and B9C. Cf. BD 130a.

^{b}B2Bo omits "eastern." Half of the preserved mss. have "western" first.

^{c}Snšw, or "double doors," cf. Allen, BD, p. 212.
^{d}Snš instead of wn
^{e}B3C omits f.
^{f}On B1Bo these last three imperatives are compressed into "Open, doors of the day bark."
^{g}Version B occurs in B1L, B2L, B3L, and B1C.
^{h}B2L repeats "leaves" here instead of using "doors." B3L has "that he may go forth from the horizon and the doors of the day bark."
^{i}Nw in B2L and B3L. N mỉ Rꜥ in B1L is probably an error but could be for mỉn "that those who are in the suite may follow him today and every day.

The first part of spell 1064 which parallels 1171 names another demon to be passed.

CT 1064 (35)

A^a [322]Its name is "Dog-face," great of form. ^{323}This which is before me is a spell for passing it.^{b}

B^c [322]Its name^d is "Great-face," great of form. ^{323}This which is on their lake^e is a spell for passing it.

CT 1171 (41')

C^f ^{513}This is a spell for passing it. It is its ⌜corpse⌝.^{g} Its name is "Dog-face," great of form.

^{a}Version A occurs in B2Bo, B4Bo, B4L, and B12C. B9C and B1C have affinities to both versions A and B.
^{b}B12C, B4L, and B9C omit this statement.
^{c}Version B occurs in B1L, B2L, and B3L.
^{d}B1C adds another pw, "This its name..."
^{e}B2L has stꜣ for sn, "which is on the aroura of land."
^{f}Version C occurs in B4L, B1P, B1Be, and B5C.
^{g}Written hỉsw, perhaps related to hỉt, cf. ECT, II 257 d. Hỉsw also occurs in CT 1064/1174 below.

The rest of spell 1064 plus 1063 parallels most of spell 1174 except its beginning. The deceased addresses a catlike demon.

Section IV

CT 1064 (35)

A[a] [323]It is a spell for the heir[b] of the message of "⌜Corpses⌝."[c] It is a spell for passing it.

B[d] [323]It is a spell for passing it.

CT 1063 (34)

A[e] ³²¹I have inherited the horizon of Re. I am indeed Lord of All. I am one who copies what has been said to him.[f] I am heir of the horizon. ³²²Make way for Re when he stops, O plunderer[g] whose name I know.

B[h] ³²¹I have inherited the horizon of Re. I am Atum, lord of Keneset.[i] I said, I inherit the horizon. ³²²Make way for Re when he stops, O heir whose name I know.

CT 1174 (44')

C[j] [514]Spell for the inheritance of the fugitive, "Face-of-⌜corpses⌝," the heir of the horizon of Re. I am Atum, lord of Kenes. I said, I am heir of the horizon. I make way for Re when he stops, O heir, whose name I know.

---

[a]Version A occurs in B3C, B12C, B2Bo, B4Bo, B4L, B9C, and B1C.

[b]ꜥwꜥw for iwꜥ generally but B9C has iwꜥ.

[c]Ḥꜣsw.

[d]Version B occurs in B1L and B3L.

[e]Version A occurs in B3C, B4C, B12C, B1Bo, B2Bo, B4Bo, and B4L. B9C has affinities to both versions A and B.

[f]B12C and B4L have ḏddt, but a passive participle with uncommon prothetic reed-leaf (cf. Edel, Alt. Gram. § 639) still makes more sense than an imperfective relative, "what I say to him."

[g]ꜥwnt.

[h]Version B occurs in B2L, B1L, B3L, and B1C.

[i]B1C has "lord of wounds."

[j]Version C occurs in B1Be, B1P, B5C, and B4L.

CT 1062 is paralleled by 1170, 1173 and the first part of 1174. In a pool surrounded by the land way, it names a demon "Hippopotamus-face," but on B1C the demon is pictured as a serpent with a bull's head.

CT 1062 (33)

A[a]   320Its name is "Hippopotamus-face," who rages (with) divine striking-force.[b] It is his ⌜corpse⌝.[c] Spell for going around by day if someone knows how to.

B[d]   320"Hippopotamus-face," who rages (with) divine striking-force. Spell for going around them by day. If someone knows this spell, he reaches this lake and he cannot die.

CT 1170 (40')

C[e]   [512]"Hippopotamus-face," awake (with) divine striking-force. Recognize it! This is its face. Its name is "⌜Corpse⌝."[f]

CT 1173 (43')

C[g]   [513]Spell for going around in a single day, if [one knows] this spell.

CT 1174 (44')

C[h]   514He reaches this lake. He cannot die.

---

[a]Version A occurs in B3C, B12C, B2Bo, B4Bo, and B4L. B9C and B1C have affinities to both versions A and B. Cf. BD 144.

[b]B9C omits 3t rn.f pw, "Hippopotamus-face, who rages." B1C has "the striking-force of Re."

[c]Written š3sw usually, B4L has št3sw and B1C has h3s. The determinative in four of the examples is a basket like the determinative of h3sw above.

[d]Version B occurs in B1L, B2L and B3L.

[e]Version C occurs in B4L, B1P, B1Be, and B5C.

[f]š3s.

Section IV

[g] This is an attempt to restore B5C. B1Be and B4L are in worse condition and B1P is apparently condensed.

[h] Version C occurs in B1Be, B1P, B5C, and B4L.

"Great-name" in spell 1061/1172 could refer to Thoth since in 1082/1085 the deceased serves Osiris as "Great-name who makes his light," and in 1093 the way of Thoth is toward the house of Maat. "Horus, the eldest son of Re," is the god who goes around the sky in CT 1104. These references provide further support for taking the map section as a cosmological plan. This lower land way represents the underworld, and all of the principle gods of the book are involved here in some way or other.

CT 1061 (32)

A[a] [317] I am "Great-name."[b] You have steered me to[c] the way of Maat. Executioners are my abomination. 318 The protection of Horus, the eldest son of Re, is my protection.[d] I am[e] the one who has acted as he wishes.[f] My foot has not been seized. I have not been opposed at the gates of the sky. 319 I am the one who has equipped Ruty,[g] Heket, and the living gods.[h] May you not destroy me.

B[i] [317] I am "Great-name." May you steer my ⟨name⟩[j] to the way of Maat. Executioners are my abomination. 318 The protection of Horus, the eldest son of Re, is my protection. (I) have done his will. I have not been seized, I have not been opposed at the gates. 319 I am the one who has equipped Ruty, Heket, and ⌜Nun⌝,[k] that I may live on the one who has destroyed him.[l]

CT 1172 (42')

C[m] [513] I am "Great-name" whom you have made. I go to the way of Maat. The place of execution is my abomination. The protection of Horus, the elder, is my protection.[n]

CT 1175 (45')

C^m [514]Horus, the eldest son of Re. I am the one who has acted as he wishes. I have not been seized. I have not^o been opposed at the regions^p and the gates. ^{515}I am the one who has equipped Ruty, who lives on the one who has destroyed him.
SPELL FOR PASSING IT. IT^q IS THE KEEPER OF THE BEND OF THE LAKE.

^{a}Version A occurs in B3C, B12C, B13C, B1Bo, B2Bo, B4Bo, and B4L. B9C has affinities to both versions A and B. Cf. BD 144.
^{b}B9C omits rn, "I am the great one."
^{c}Cf. CDME, p. 27, for ir . . . hr.
^{d}B12C omits mk.i pw. B4L omits smsw.
^{e}The scribe of B3C failed to change the subject to 3rd person "This N." here, so B3C also has ink.
^{f}N ib.f, or, "because of his will."
^{g}B12C has ntrw "gods" for Rwty.
^{h}Or perhaps, "I am equipped. O Ruty, Heket, and the living gods, may you not destroy me." Zandee, Death, p. 185, suggests "is equipped with . . . ."
^{i}Version B occurs in B1L, B2L, B3L, and B1C.
^{j}B1C and B2L have an s before rn (?) and the reading of B1L is uncertain.
^{k}Nun is probably intended on B1C, but it is uncertain on B1L and B3L and omitted on B2L.
^{l}B1L has iw for sw.
^{m}Version C occurs in B1Be, B1P, B5C, and B4L.
^{n}The spell is similarly translated by Zandee, Death, p. 170.
^{o}Nn for n in B1Be.
^{p}B1P omits w'rwt.
^{q}B5C has pw pw, "THIS IS..."

The picture that we get from the text of CT 1060/1169 is of the journey of the solar bark through the underworld past another demon. The deceased is of course pilot of the solar bark.

Section IV

CT 1060 (31)

A[a] [313] I have come here from the numbering of the horizon [314] that I may herald[b] Re at the gates of the sky, and that the gods may rejoice in meeting me. The odor of god (goes) toward me.[c] [315] The evil-ones[d] have not reached me and the keepers of the gates have not excluded me. I am the secret one in the midst of the chapel, [316] who is over the[e] shrine of the one who has been bound. This is the chapel which I have reached [317] in the land of tombs.

B[f] [313] I have come here from the holy place[g] of the horizon of the sky [314] that I may herald[b] Re at the gates of the sky.[h] Rejoice, O gods, in meeting me. The odor of god[i] (goes) toward me.[c] [315] The evil-ones have not reached me and the keepers of the gates have not excluded me. I am "Secret-of-face" in the midst of the palace,[j] [316] who was over the shrine of the god[k] at the time when I reached it after Hathor had purified herself. The chapel was enfolded[l] at the time when I reached [317] the land of tombs.

CT 1169 (39')

C[m] [511] I have come here from primeval time that I may herald[b] Re at the gates of the sky. Rejoice, O gods, in meeting me. The odor of god (goes) toward me. The evil-one cannot reach me and the keepers of the rooms[n] cannot destroy me.[o] I was "Secret-of-face" in the midst of a chapel [512] at the time when I reached it[p] after Hathor had purified the shrine of the god who binds. THIS WHICH IS BEFORE IS A SPELL FOR [q] PASSING IT. UNDER THIS LAKE IS THE NAME OF THIS BEND. IT WAS THE GUARDIAN OF THIS LAKE at the time when I reached it in the land of ⟨tombs⟩,[r] the mansions of the ⌜red-crown⌝.[s]

[a] Version A occurs in B3C, B12C, B13C, B1Bo, B2Bo, B4Bo, B4L, and B4C. B9C has affinities to both versions A and B. Cf. BD 144g.

[b] Sr, or, "reach." With the walking-legs determinative in versions B and C, this meaning seems more likely intended there.

^cOr, "is against."

^d<u>Nbdw</u>.

^eB4L has "his."

^fVersion B occurs in B1L, B2L, B3L, and B1C.

^g<u>Dsrw</u> for <u>dsrw</u>?

^hB3L has <u>ȝḥt</u>, "horizon," for <u>pt</u>.

ⁱB9C has "the gods."

^jOr, "temple." <u>ꜥḥ</u> in all but B3L which has <u>ḥwt ꜥȝt</u>.

^kB9C has "of the gods." Cf. Allen, <u>BD</u>, p. 233, note ai.

^l<u>Kȝb</u> in B1L and B2L, <u>kȝs</u> "was bound" in B1C.

^mVersion C occurs in B4L, B1P, B1Be, and B5C.

ⁿB1Be has <u>ꜥ[w]t</u> "rooms." B4L has <u>ꜥwt</u> "limbs." The word is illegible on B5C and B1P.

^oB4L omits <u>w</u> of <u>wȝ</u>.

^pOn B1P the spell ends here.

^qB4L omits <u>r n</u>.

^r<u>Bꜥt</u> for <u>wꜥbt</u>?

^sSuggested by de Buck for the traces in B4L. If this proposed restoration is correct, it could indicate that this was originally a text from Lower Egypt.

CT 1168 begins with the names of two keepers. The second of these is paralleled by CT 1057 and the rest of the spell is paralleled by CT 1058. The difficult first name in 1168 is probably paralleled by CT 1059. The keeper in spell 1059 is a quadruped holding a dagger. It has a reed leaf on top of its human head with its face turned backwards. The name is also written before CT 1060 on B4Bo. Spell 1057 names another keeper pictured in B1C as a hare with a knife. In CT 1058 the deceased is said to repel the opposition of the aggressors, presumably from his position at the prow of the sun bark.

CT 1059 (30)

A,B^a [312] Its^b name is "Protector-of-the-two-gods." [313] This is the keeper of the bend. It is the guardian who goes down in it.^c

Section IV

CT 1057 (28)

A[d] [309] "Sharp-one,"[e] the keeper of the lake. This is the keeper of the bend.

B[f] [309] Its name is "Sharp-of-face," the keeper of the lake. This is the keeper of the bend.

CT 1058 (29)

A[g] ³¹⁰I am the one who repels the opposition[h] of the aggressors, who travels, and who ⌜flies up⌝.[i] (I am) the one who is beneath the egg,[j] whose dignity is here (when) he appears in early morning. ³¹¹His dignity is guarded[k] because I have attained it.[l] When he appears, I see him.[m] Delay is my abomination, since I know him. ³¹²He has not lived in the horizon. He has excluded[n] me and the young god.

B[o] ³¹⁰I am the one who repels the opposition of the aggressors, who travels, and who flies up. I am the one who is beneath the egg of Re, whose dignity is here when he appears in early morning. ³¹¹He and his dignity are guarded by the one who has attacked it.[p] Delay is my abomination[q] since I know him.[r] ³¹²He has not lived in the horizon having opposed me and my young local god.

CT 1168 (38')

C[s] ⁵¹⁰ITS NAME IS "⌜Divine-Ka,⌝"[t] (whose) form came into being.⌝[u] IT IS THE KEEPER OF THE BEND OF THE LAKE. ITS NAME IS "SHARP-FACE." THIS IS THE FLAME WHICH IS ON IT.[v] I am the one who repels the two opponents of the aggressors, who walks rather than runs.[w] I am the one who is beneath the egg of Re whose dignity is here[x] when he appears in early morning. His dignity was guarded for me[y] that I might reach it. Flesh is my abomination. Those who are in the horizon go forth[z] hastening. ⁵¹¹Since I know that he is[aa] in the horizon, I and my young god, Khekhet,[ab] are opposed.[ac]

^aThis name occurs in B3C, B12C, B13C, B2Bo, B4Bo^{a,b}, B4L, B9C, B1C, B1L, B2L, B3L, and B4C. Cf. Zandee, Death, p. 129, for his translation of the spell.

^bB12 has "This its name."

^cOr, "guardian of the one who goes down in it."

^dVersion A occurs in B3C, B12C, B13C, B2Bo, B4Bo, and B4L. Cf. BD 144.

^eMds, B4Bo has sds in error.

^fVersion B occurs in B1L, B2L, B3L, B1C, and B9C.

^gVersion A occurs in B3C, B12C, B13C, B1Bo, B2Bo, B4Bo, and B4L. B9C has affinities to both versions A and B.

^hB12C, B13C, and B4L have "the two opponents" or "who repels the opponent, who opposes the aggressors."

ⁱMss. with Version A have irtt but mss. with Version B have itt "fly up."

^jB12C omits swht.

^kB12C, B1Bo, and B2Bo have the passive sdm.f form and are therefore past tense.

^lB4L has "I have not attained it." B12C has the same or "There is no one who has attained it."

^mB12C, B13C, and B4L have "When he appeared, I did not see him."

ⁿWritten hmwt.f wi with a very troublesome t.

^oVersion B occurs in B1L, B2L, B3L, and B1C.

^pOr "He is guarded. (As for) his dignity, can it be that (I) reach it?"

^qHere B9C adds "I have not seen him."

^rB3L omits sw.

^sVersion C occurs in B4L, B1P, B5C, and B1Be.

^tWritten k-ntr, k for ki?

^uHpr hpr(w) or hprwi in B1Be and B5C; plural in B1P; and omitted by B4L.

^vCf. Zandee, Death, p. 246, for a slightly different rendering of the last three statements.

^wBtt.

^xB1P has "like that of Re" instead of "here."

^yOr, "Guard his dignity for me."

^zWritten pr hr sw for which I propose pr.hr imyw. B5C ends here.

^{aa}The independent pronoun swt is used as subject of a sentence with adverbial predicate.

^{ab}Or possibly a corruption of niwty, "local."

^{ac}So in B1P and B4L but perhaps this should have been either active or negative.

Section IV

The land way ends with spell 1056,1055/1167 in de Buck's edition. The references to "lake" occur in the spaces around the land way and give us the picture of inundation with black roadways on earthen dikes separating bodies of water. The request to make way for the deceased to sail the bark does not seem to pertain to the land way, however, the bark could be towed from the land as it is e.g. in the Book of Amduat (4th and 5th hours).

CT 1056 (27)

A,B^a 309"Great-face"^{b} who opposes the aggressors is^c the keeper^d of this bend.

CT 1055 (26)

A,B^a 307A spell for passing it is that which is beneath this lake.^{e} Let me pass peacefully. Make way for me that I may sail the bark. 308His^f protection is my protection. That which will happen to me, the like will happen to him,^{g} if you act.^{h}

CT 1167 (37')

C^i 509"Great-face" who opposes the aggressors is its name. This is a spell for enfolding it.^{j} A spell for passing it is that which is beneath this lake. May I cause that I pass^k peacefully that Re may proceed.^{l} Make way for me that he^m may sail and that he may proceed. The protection of Re is my protection.^{n} Everything which will happen^o to me, the like will happen to Re, if anything is done against me. I am the one who opposes the aggressors.

^{a}Version A occurs in B3C, B12C, B13C, B1Bo, B2Bo, B4Bo, and B4L. B1Bo omits the heading. Version B occurs in B1L, B2L, B3L, B2P, and B1C. B9C has affinities to both versions. Cf. BD 144.

^{b}B1C has "Cursed-face."

^{c}Version B including B9C adds "the name of."

^{d}B13C has i͗tr for i͗ry and B4L has i͗trw!

ᵉB1Bo and B9C omit this sentence. B13C and B12C seem to have "garden." B13C, B2Bo, and B4L have hr.f and B3C has n̲ for f̲ erroneously. These can be read "beneath him and this lake" or "beneath him. It is a lake." In the second case this would be merely a label for the pool beside the land way.

ᶠB2L has "Re's."

ᵍB12C omits mitt ir.f. Version A has the old writing ir.f (irr.f in B4L) while B-version has r.f.

ʰOr, "since you have acted." B-version excluding B9C has "since you have done everything to me. I am the one who opposes the aggressors." B2L also has dw, "evilly."

ⁱVersion C occurs in B4L, B1P, B1Be, and B5C.

ʲThis survives only on B4L.

ᵏB4L has "Let me pass."

ˡB4L has "be sound."

ᵐA seated-man is written after f̲ in B4L erroneously.

ⁿCf. Zandee's translation of the last three sentences in Death, p. 27.

ᵒB4L has "that which will happen."

SECTION V

Section V is introduced by CT 1180 in the C-version and this is paralleled by part of CT 1052. This new section involves specifically the "ways of Rosetaw" which are on land and water.

CT 1052 (23)

B[a] [304]Mysterious serpents, keepers of the gates.

CT 1180 (50')

C[b] 518Mysterious serpents, keepers of the gates, keepers of my way.

[a]Version B occurs in B1C, B1L, and B2L.
[b]Version C occurs in B1Be, B1P. and B5C.

Spell 1070 on the B-version coffins labels the flaming walls that divide spell 1071 into three compartments. Spell 1071 is addressed to a group of "watchers" who are depicted on B1C. They are ordered to prostrate themselves before the deceased. The top compartment of the three that contain the spell names a demon, and its name is the spell for passing it. The other two compartments also contain the names of demons and groups. The deceased as Re, "the companion of Thoth," is on the solar bark, "Eye of Horus," before Hu and Sia, the other gods at the back of the solar bark in Spell 1128.

CT 1070 (41) and 1071 (42)

A[a] 334"High-of-winds" is its name. This which is beneath it[b] is a spell for passing it.[c] "Lord-of-divine-striking-force" is its name. O watchmen,[d] 335I am loud-of-voice in the horizon, a great one like[e] you.[f] On your faces, O watchmen, make way for your[g] lord. It is I. "Blazer"[h] is its name.[i] 336This which is beneath it[j] is a

spell for passing it.^j "Flaming-faces"^k is its name. O lords of might, my face is (as) the Great-ones's. ^337My back is (as) the great crown's. I am lord of those of might.^l
"⌜Morbid⌝^m-of-form" is its name. This which is beneath it is a spell for passing it. ^338"⌜Serpent⌝^n-face" is its name. "Lord-of-breezes"^o is its name. I am the one who sits on the "Eye-of-Horus" as the first of three,^p whom the gods judge^q as the companion of Thoth. ^339The protection of Thoth is^r my protection with you.^s

B^t   [333]It is flame that opposes one.
^334"High-of-⌜flesh-^u and⌝-winds," equipped. This which is beneath it^v is a spell for passing it. "Lord-of-divine-striking force." O watchmen, ^335 I am loud-of-voice in the horizon, like the Great-one. On your faces, O watchmen, make way for your lord. It is I.
[333]It is flame that opposes one.
[335]"Blazer" is its name. ^336This which is beneath them is a spell for passing it. "Flame" is its name. My face is (as) the Great-one's. ^337My back is (as) the great crown's. To me belongs might.
[333]It is flame that opposes one.
[337]"⌜Morbid⌝-of-form" is its name. This which is beneath them is a spell for passing it. ^338"⌜Serpent⌝-face," "⌜Those-who-are-twisted⌝."^w I am the one who sits on the eye, the third person,^x who is judged as the companion of Thoth. ^339The protection of Thoth is my protection with you.

CT 1181 (51')

C^y   [518]Spell for passing it. "High-of-equipment." "Lord-of-divine-striking-force." I am loud-of-voice in the horizon, its Great-one. On your faces, O watchmen.
A spell for passing it. My face is (as) Horus'. My back is (as) the great crown's. Mine is might.
Spell for passing it. I am the one who sits on the "Eye-of-Horus" as the third, ^519who is judged among the gods as a companion in the day. The protection of Thoth (is) my protection with you.

Section V

^aVersion A occurs in B3C, B4C, B12C, B13C, B2Bo, B4Bo, and B4L. B9C and B1C have affinities to both versions A and B. Cf. BD 144 and 147b.

^bB3C and B4C have <u>sn</u> "them" for <u>s</u>. B4Bo has <u>f</u>, "him" or "it."

^cB12C and B4Bo have <u>f</u>, "him" or "it" for <u>s</u>.

^dB12C, B13C, and B4L omit all of the above except the second sentence.

^eꜣIs, cf. Edel, <u>Alt. Gram.</u>, II, §828, for this use of the enclitic particle.

^fB9C omits <u>tn</u>.

^gB13C and B4L have <u>mw</u> for <u>tn</u> in error, due to similarity in writing.

^hBsy, cf. Hornung, <u>Amduat</u>, II, 28.

ⁱB12C, B13C, and B4L omit this sentence.

^jB12C and B4L have <u>f</u>, "him" or "it," for <u>s</u>.

^kB9C has <u>sdt r</u> instead of <u>sdt hrw</u> apparently in error, and B9C also added a brazier and seated god determinative after <u>pw</u>. Perhaps we should read "Flame is his name" as in version B.

^lWsrwt, cf. CT 1034 note d above. B4C ends here and B2C skips through to "I am one who sits . . ."

^mHꜣsf (?)

ⁿWritten hꜣf for hfꜣ.

^oNꜣw, but B12C has ꜣtw "aggressors."

^pB12C and B4L add "every day." Cf. Allen <u>BD</u>, p. 252, notes v and w. "Eye of Horus" is probably the name of the bark here, rather than "throne" as Allen suggests.

^qB9C and B1C have "who is judged."

^rB9C and B3C omit the sentence pronoun <u>pw</u>.

^sM-ꜥ.tn; or, "and yours."

^tVersion B occurs in B1L, B2L, B3L, and B2P. The three labels of CT 1070 occur on B1L, B2L, and B1C, while the label occurs only once on B3L, B9C, and B2P.

^uꜣIwf; B1C has kꜣ.s tꜣw rn.f pw "It (fem.) is high. Its (masc.) name is 'Winds'."

^vB2L has "them."

^wNhꜣw. After this B9C adds "they see ⸢the protector (hꜣ)⸣ on the roads."

^xTp hmt-nw, or perhaps it should be "as the first of three."

^yVersion C occurs in B1Be, B1P, and B5C.

Spell 1072/1182 is an explanation of the ways of Rosetaw. Although it is not perfectly clear, it seems that it is best interpreted as indicating that the ways should continue one another.

CT 1072 (43)

A[a] [339]Spell for the ways of this Rosetaw which are on water and land.[b] These ways are here [340]in the opposite direction,[c] each one thereof opposing its companion in the opposite direction. It is those who know them[d] who can find their ways. [341]They are high on the walls of flint.[e]

B[f] [339]Flame. Spell for the way of[g] Rosetaw. These ways and the end of those ways [340] are in the opposite direction, one opposing its companion. If they know how to find their way, [341]the walls of flint are high in[h] Rosetaw on water and on land.

CT 1182 (52')

C[i] [519]IT IS THE SPELL FOR THE WAY.[j] THESE WAYS ARE LIKE THIS: ONE THEREOF OPPOSING ITS COMPANION IN THE OPPOSITE DIRECTION. AS FOR THE ONES WHO KNOW THEM, THEY CAN FIND THEIR WAYS. THE HEIGHT OF THE WALLS[k] OF FLINT IS IN ROSETAW.

- - - - - - - - - - - - - - -

[a]Version A occurs in B3C, B4C, B2Bo, and B4Bo. B9C has affinities to both versions A and B.

[b]For the A-version, the phrase in ECT, VII 341 b, probably should continue ECT, VII 339 e, as de Buck suggested. The nt and the hrt would both depend on "ways." B4Bo repeats nt r-st3w erroneously and B9C has "Spell for the ways of Rosetaw. Its ways end by travelling." B1C has "spell for the way of Rosetaw," without pn hrt mw t].

[c]Stnm, or "in confusion."

[d]B3C and B4C have s, "it," for sn.

[e]Dsw, or "knives."

[f]Version B occurs in B1L, B2L, B3L, B2P, and B1C.

[g]B2L has r "to."

[h]B3L has "which are in."

[i]Version C occurs in B1Be, B1P, and B5C.

[j]Cf. Zandee, Death, p. 165, for a somewhat similar translation of the whole spell.

[k]B1P has "their walls."

Section V

In spell 1073/1183 the deceased confronts the "squatters" who were equated with "keepers" in CT 1053/1165. In this spell the deceased attends Osiris so that he (A and probably C=deceased; B=Osiris) can watch the passage of Re.

CT 1073 (44)

A[a] ^{342}Be weary, O squatters, hidden of faces, living by their throwsticks.[b] I am mighty, ^{343}weighty[c] of divine striking force, who made his way from the flame. I have treated Osiris. Make way for me that I may pass. ^{344}Then I shall see the unique one who goes around, Re, among those who made offerings. Make way for me. ^{345}Let me pass very safely.

B[d] ^{342}Be weary, O squatters, hidden of faces, living by their ⌜throwsticks⌝.[e] I am mighty of heart, ^{343}weighty of divine striking force, one who made his way from the flame. I have treated Osiris. Make way for me. Let me pass ^{344}that I may preserve Osiris so that he may see the unique one who goes around, Re, among those who made offerings.

CT 1183 (53')

C[f] ^{520}Be weary, O squatters, hidden of faces, living by their throwsticks and their ⌜sticks⌝.[g] Mighty[h] of heart, weighty of divine striking force, who made[i] (his) way from the flame. I have treated Osiris. Make way for me. Let me pass. I am the one who preserves Osiris, who sees the unique one, who goes around Re, among those who act alone.

[a]Version A occurs in B3C, B4C, B12C, B13C, B1Bo, B2Bo, and B4Bo. B9C and B1C have affinities to both versions A and B. Cf. BD 147b.

[b]Cf. Allen, BD, p. 252, note z.

[c]B12C has a dittography after this which goes back to "their throwsticks."

[d]Version B occurs in B1L, B2L, B3L, and B2P.

[e]M(ꜣ)t.

[f]Version C occurs in B1Be, B1P, and B5C.

[g]Ḥw(w), or "throwsticks which strike the neck (wsrt)."

^{h}Written wsrt. B1P ends here.
^{i}B5C omits ir. B1Be omits it.

The land way of Rosetaw is labeled by spell 1074/1184, and in this section the land way is clearly on top. In 1075/1184 the deceased is the "one who parted the two companions." The two companions are again probably Re and Thoth, as sun and moon, rather than Horus and Seth. The deceased also serves Osiris here.

CT 1074 (45)

A,B^a [345]The ways of Rosetaw which are on land.

CT 1075 (46)

A,B^a ^{346}I am the one who fixed the limits^b of the flood, who parted the two companions. I have come that I may remove the lowness^d upon^e Osiris.

CT 1184 (54')

C^f [520]I am the one who split^g you, who parted the two companions. I have come that I may remove the lowness upon Osiris.
^{521}THE WAY OF ROSETAW WHICH IS ON LAND.

^{a}This occurs in B3C, B4C, B12C, B13C, B2Bo, B4Bo, B1C, B9C, B1L, B2L, and B2P. B2Bo, B2L, and B2P are rubricized. Cf. BD 147c, 4.
^{b}B12C has šti "hid" for tiš.
^{c}Or, less likely, "who judged."
^{d}Written dhw and dhw.
^{e}Or, "from."
^{f}Version C occurs in B1P, B1Be, and B5C.
^{g}Written tišbw for tšb? Or, "smashed," cf. CDME p. 301.

Spells 1076 and 1077 are lists of names of various of the inhabitants of the underworld according to versions A and B respectively.

Section V

CT 1076 (47)

A^a [346]"One who spits out the Nile."^b "One who has given itself." 347"One who confers attributes."^c "One who eats its fathers." "One who eats its mothers." "One who opposes angry Seth." "One who has begotten the bull of Heliopolis." "One who has swallowed the chaos-gods."^d The face of the falcon has gone forth from Uto. The (four) faces have gone forth from the horizon.

^aThese names occur in B3C, B4C, B2Bo, B4Bo, and B1C.
^bB1C adds "is its name."
^cNhb-k3w, the well known serpent deity.
^dḤḥw, cf. Faulkner, PT, p. 133, note 8.

CT 1077 (48)

B^a [347]"Numerous of faces" who hears the ⌈cobra-goddesses⌉.^b "Chatterer." "⌈Cobra-goddess⌉."^c "One who encounters the cow." 348"One who ignores^d Khepri." "One who stretches out (its) legs."^e "⌈Cobra-goddess⌉."^c "One who catches a multitude."

^aThese names occur in B1L, B2L, B2P, and B9C.
^bDȝdwt with a cobra determinative.
^cB9C has "cobra-god."
^dWȝh.
^eB2P has the dual; the other mss. have "leg."

The order of the remaining spells in this section is determined by the fact that the last spells of version A (1078, 1079, 1080, 1081, and 1082) parallel and correspond exactly to the order of the last spells in version C (1185, 1086, 1087, and 1085). In version B the spells from one source are followed by those from the other. The repetition of the variant endings to this section shows us that version B is dependent on A and C.

The waterway of Rosetaw is labeled in CT 1078/1185, and 1079/1185 includes a list of the deceased's activities. Rosetaw, perhaps originally the Memphitic necropolis associated with the god Sokar, is here incidentally but clearly connected with the Osirian necropolis of Abydos. The rubric in version A describes the "kneelers" as the guards placed around Osiris to protect him from his brother, Seth. These are again the demon keepers whose names the deceased must know. Spell 1086 has a new heading, "wall of charcoal," apparently not designating anything pictured.

CT 1078 (49)

A,B^a [348] The ways of Rosetaw on water.^{b}

CT 1079 (50)

A^c [348] I am the one who dressed his standard, ^{349}who went forth from the great crown. I have come that I may establish offerings in Abydos. I opened^d Rosetaw that I may heal^e the malady of Osiris. ^{350}I am the one who brought water into being, who assigned^f his standard, who made his way in the valley of the Great-one. Make a shining way for me. Let me pass, ^{351}that I may remove pain from the one who made himself.^{g} AS FOR THESE SQUATTERS, IT IS^h GEB WHO HAS ESTABLISHED THEM IN ROSETAW IN REACH OF HIS SON OSIRIS FOR FEAR OF HIS BROTHER, SETH, LEST HE HARM HIM. AS FOR ANY PERSON WHO KNOWS THE NAME(S) OF THESE SQUATTERS, HE WILL BE WITH OSIRIS FOREVER. HE CAN NEVER PERISH.

B^i [348] I am the one who dressed his standard, ^{349}who went forth from the great crown. I have come that I may establish offerings in Abydos. Rosetaw has been opened that I may heal the malady of Osiris. ^{350}I am the one who brought water into being, who assigned his standard, who made his way^j in the valley of the Great-one. Make a shining^k way for me. Let me pass that I may remove lingering^l and that I may heal the sickness in Osiris.

CT 1185 (55')

C^m [521] I am the one who dressed the standard, who went forth

Section V

from the great crown. I have come that I may remove pain, that I may heal the pains^n in Osiris, and that I may establish offerings in Abydos.
THE WAYS OF ROSETAW WHICH ARE ON WATER.

CT 1086 (57)

B^o [362]They are the walls of charcoal.
Open the way in Rosetaw ^{363}that I may heal the malady for Osiris. I am the one who caused to come to be that which exists,^{p} who assigned his standard, and who made his way in the valley of the Great-one. Make a shining way for me. ^{364}Let me pass.

C^p [362]It is a wall of charcoal.
I open the way in Rosetaw. ^{363}I heal the malady for Osiris. I am the one who caused to come to be that which exists, who assigned his standard, who made his^r way in the valley of the Great-one. Make way for me that I may remove its light. ^{364}Let me pass.

^{a}This occurs in B3C, B12C, B13C, B2Bo, B4Bo, B1C, B9C, B1L, and B2L.

^{b}B2Bo and B2L are rubricized.

^{c}Version A occurs in B3C, B12C, B13C, B2Bo, B4Bo, and B9C. B1C is illegible for the most part but has affinities to both versions A and B. Cf. BD 147c and 117.

^{d}B3C without n has "that I may open."

^{e}B4Bo has "after N. has healed."

^{f}Wdf.

^{g}B13C concludes the upper register here and the lower register is lost. B12C and B9C end the spell here, so the rubric continues in only B3C, B4Bo, B1C, and in B2Bo the text occurs unrubricized. Cf. Allen, BD, p. 192 note h, top.

^{h}B3C omits i of in.

^{i}Version B occurs in B1L, B2L, and B3L.

^{j}The spell ends here on B3L.

^{k}B1L has snt for sšp.

^{l}Ihm, or "mourning."

^{m}Version C occurs in B1Be, B1P, and B5C.

^{n}Mrt instead of mnt.

°Version B occurs in B1L, B2L, and B3L. Cf. BD 147a.

ᵖCT 1079 (ECT, VII 350 a) had mw "water" for ntt, an error in writing.

ᑫVersion C occurs in B5C, and twice each in B1Be and B1P.

ʳB5C omits f.

Spell 1080 refers to a sealed place in darkness surrounded by flame and containing the effluvium of Osiris. Spell 1081 is supposed to prevent any person seen there from perishing. The parallel text in version C, which was repeated in version B, has "speech (mdt)" for "sealed place (htmt)" and if this "speech" is known, it is a guarantee of life, breath, and the daily vision of Osiris. The distinction between "spirit" and "person" is probably significant as indicating that the work would be useful whether acquired before or after death.

CT 1080 (51)

A,Bᵃ 352This isᵇ the sealed place which is in the midst ofᶜ darknessᵈ. Flameᵈ is around it containing thisᵉ effluvium of Osiris. It was placed inᶠ Rosetaw. 353It has been concealed since it fell from him.ᵍ It is what descended from him upon the land of sand. That which has been placedʰ in Rosetaw is what exists under him.ⁱ

CT 1081 (52)

A,Bʲ 354As for any person who is seen there alive,ᵏ he can never perish since he knowsˡ the spell for passing by theᵐ squatters, the keepers of the gates.

CT 1087 (58)

B,Cⁿ [364]THIS IS THE SPEECH WHICH IS IN THE MIDST OF DARKNESS. AS FOR ANY SPIRIT WHO KNOWS IT, IT (spirit) LIVES AMONG THE LIVING. FLAME IS AROUND IT (the speech) CONTAINING THIS EFFLUVIUM OF OSIRIS. 365AS FOR ANY PERSON WHO WILL KNOW IT,° HE CAN NEVER° PERISH THERE SINCE HE KNOWS WHAT WILL EXIST INᵖ ROSETAW. ROSETAW IS HIDDEN SINCE HE FELL THEREIN

Section V

HAVING DESCENDED[q] FROM UPON THE HILL-COUNTRY.[r] WHAT IS UNDER HIM IN BUSIRIS IS WRITING MATERIALS. ROSETAW IS THE CORRUPTION OF OSIRIS. AS FOR ANY PERSON WHO IS THERE, 366 HE SEES OSIRIS EVERY DAY. BREATH IS IN HIS NOSE.[s] HE CAN NEVER DIE,[t] since he knows the spell for passing it.

[a] Version A occurs in B3C, B4C, B12C, B2Bo, and B4Bo. Version B occurs in B1L, B2L, and B2P. B9C has affinities to both versions A and B.

[b] B-version omits nw.

[c] B-version has m hnw abbreviated to the cow's-skin (rather than goat-skin) and nw-jar which on B2L and B2P looks more like a sun-disk.

[d] On B1L the text ends here.

[e] B-version omits pw.

[f] B12C apparently has "It was repelled from."

[g] B3C has hr.f im.s "it fell from her." B4C, B12C, and B2Bo have "since it (s) fell from him (f)," or for B4C perhaps "since she fell on it." B4Bo omits final f. B9C has final s. In B2L both pronouns are f. Cf. Zandee, Death, p. 89 for a different translation of this much of the spell.

[h] B-version has "that which is heavy/offered (wdnt)" instead of wdyt.

[i] Or, "in his possession."

[j] Version A occurs in B3C, B4C, B12C, B2Bo, and B4Bo. Version B occurs in B1L and B2L which are rubricized.

[k] ʿnh is omitted in B-version.

[l] B12C has ndr.hr.f "Then he grasps" for dr rh.f.

[m] B4Bo and B-version have ipw "those" and the B-version omits "the keepers of the gates."

[n] Version B occurs in B2L, B3L and probably B1L. Version C occurs in B5C and twice each in B1Be and B1P.

[o] B5C omits s and n, a haplography.

[p] B2L and B3L omit s of wn.t(y).s(y) and the following m.

[q] iw(.f) hi.

[r] B2L omits hist.

[s] B-version mss. omit "Every day. Breath is in his nose." B2L omitted rubrics for this and the last sentence.

[t] Version B concludes here.

Spell 1083 (54) labels a door as "Flame" on B1L alone. Part of spell 1084 belongs with spell 577 which ends this section, but the last two headings of 1084 parallel the beginning of 1085 in version C. Spell 1082 in version A is a partial parallel for spell 1085 in versions B and C. It is a spell for existing in Rosetaw in the service of Osiris.

CT 1082 (53)

A[a] [354]SPELL FOR EXISTING IN ROSETAW.[b]
I am Great-name who made his light. I have come to you,[c] Osiris, [355]that I may worship you and that I may cause that your effluvium raise itself.[d]

CT 1084 (55)

B[e] [356]Travelling in peace toward the palace[f] of Osiris. Passing the gates.

CT 1085 (56)

B[g] [356]Spell for existing in Rosetaw and living on the abundance of offerings[h] beside Osiris.[i] [357]I am Great-name who made his light. I have come to you, Osiris, that I may worship you.[j] You have not placed me[358]that I may cause your effluvium which flows from you to raise itself,[k] and that I may make the name of Rosetaw since I fell in it.[l] Hail to you, Osiris. [359]Raise yourself, be powerful,[m] be mighty. Be powerful in this your power of Rosetaw, [360]and in this your might of Abydos, that the unique one may go around,[361]that Re may make the circuit, and that you, Osiris, may say that[o] I am a dignitary of God. [362]I say, and it happens. I have not been kept away from you, O Re.

C[p] [356]Travelling in peace to protect[q] Osiris and passing all the gates. [357]I am Great-name who made his light. I have come to you, Osiris, that I may worship you, that I may become clean through[r] your effluvium, [358]which I have raised, and that I may make the name of Rosetaw since I fell in it. Hail to you, Osiris. [359]I raise you in your power, in your might, in life, prosperity and health. May you be powerful in Rosetaw; [360]may you be mighty in Abydos. He has turned your forehead toward the sky of Re,[s] that

Section V

you may see all the common folk. ^{361}O unique one, may you call to Re while sweeping the sky as he goes around the horizon. I speak like Osiris, for I am his mighty dignitary.^{t} ^{362}I speak and it happens as when he speaks.^{u} I have not been kept away from you, Osiris.^{v}

^{a}Version A occurs in B3C, B12C, B2Bo, and B4Bo.
^{b}This title occurs in B3C alone.
^{c}B2Bo omits k.
^{d}Or "him." B12C omits dỉ.f "and raise him up to your effluvium."
^{e}This occurs in B1L twice and once in B2L.
^{f}Stp-sỉ.
^{g}Version B occurs twice each in B1L and B2L. It also occurs in B3L, B9C, and B2P. B9C, B1L^b and B2L^b, and B2P have affinities to both versions B and C. Cf. BD 147a, 147g, and 119.
^{h}B1L^a has hỉ ht "living around the offerings" instead of m hỉw ht.
^{i}So in B2L^a but B1L adds mỉỉ and leaves a blank space after it "who sees (blank)." These are the only coffins with this introduction.
^{j}B2L^b has kw for tw in error.
^{k}Or "him." B9C has "that I may raise him and your effluvium."
^{l}Written f generally, but s in B9C.
^{m}B3L omits the next few phrases until VII 360a.
^{n}B3L has "and that Osiris may say to you."
^{o}B9C has "O unique one who makes the circuit like Re when Osiris says . . ."
^{p}Version C occurs in B5C, B1Be, and twice in B1P.
^{q}R stp-sỉ r, or "to the palace ⟨of⟩," as in CT 1084.
^{r}W‛b.ỉ n.
^{s}Or "O Re." B9C, B1L^b, B2L^b, and B2P have "May your forehead go around the sky opposite Re."
^{t}B5C has bỉ "soul"; other mss. have s‛h. B1L^b has "I am his dignitary, I am his mighty one."
^{u}B1L^b has mỉ dd.n.f "as he said."
^{v}B9C omits the god's name.

This section and the whole book were certainly concluded in version C with spells 513 and 577. These spells also occur within the Book of Two Ways on all the coffins with version B, and they occur elsewhere on two coffins with version A. CT 513 lists more claims of the deceased and he asks a doorkeeper of "this great warship" to make way for him.

CT 513

A[a] [VI 97 i] My decay[b] was caused yesterday ^{98} and I have come here. Make way for me that I may go forth and that I may take what Anubis bewailed. I am tousled[c] ^{99} having gone forth from his horizon.[d] I am disheveled having gone forth from his scepter. I am[e] lord of his white crown.[f] I am the "Third" of magic ^{100} in the protection of Maat. I am the red-one, the protection of his eye. I died yesterday, I came in the morning, I raised myself today, ^{101} and I came here. Make way for me, O doorkeeper of the great battlefield.

B[g] [97] (My) decay was caused yesterday ^{98} and I have come here (repeat). Make way for me that I may go content, that I may go after Anubis has bewailed.[h] I am tousled ^{99} having gone forth from his horizon. I am disheveled having gone forth from his scepter.[i] I am lord of the great crown. I am the "Third" of magic ^{100} in the protection of Maat. I am the protection of his[j] eye. When I have been rescued, ^{101} make way for me,[k] his doorkeeper and the great warship,

C¹ [97] (My) decay was caused yesterday ^{98} and I have come here. Make way for me (repeat), that I may be content and go after Anubis has bewailed. I am tousled ^{99} having gone forth from his horizon. I am disheveled having gone forth from his scepter. I am lord of his great crown. I am the "Third" of magic ^{100} in the protection of Maat. I am the protection of his eye. After I had been taken away yesterday, I raised myself today. ^{101} Make way for me, O doorkeeper of this great warship,

[a]Version A occurs in B9C and B1Bo. Cf. BD 179a.
[b]Wst.
[c]Sps, cf. CDME, p. 223.

^{d}B1Bo has "standard."

^{e}B1Bo omits this.

^{f}B1Bo has "great crown."

^{g}Version B occurs in B1L and B2P. B2L has affinities to both versions B and C.

^{h}B2P ends here.

^{i}B1L has <u>hd</u> "mace" for <u>shm</u>.

^{j}B1L has <u>f</u> before <u>irt</u>.

^{k}B1L has "when I cut out the way."

^{l}Version C occurs in B1Be, B5C, and twice in B1P.

In CT 577 the deceased identifies himself with Osiris and asks to go forth on this day against his enemy. It is stated at the end that "this book was under the flanks of Khnum." The only other reference to Khnum was in the introduction to the C-version (1131) where the deceased was said to be a ⌜defiant-one⌝ of Khnum. CT 577 apparently continues 513 in the middle of a sentence. There are also connections between 577 and 1053/1153. CT 1084 parallels the central portion of spell 577.

CT 577

B^a VI 192 that I may go forth in the day against my enemy and that I may be powerful over him.^{b} He has been given to me in the council. The way of the greatest of the gods^c has given him to me.

C^d VI 192 that I may go forth in the day against my enemy and that I may be powerful over him. He has been given to me. He has not been taken away from me. He is completely under me in the council. The first great mound, "power of the gods," has given him to me. He belongs to my nails like the lion. ^{193}He belongs to my palm like the crocodile. Make way for me that I may carry off my enemy. I am Osiris hiding his throne; the Foremost of the Westerners giving heads. I am the lord of blood on the days of becoming.^{e} I am lord of the sharp-ones.^{f} I have not robbed. Make way for me in front of the temple. I embalm^g

those who are in sweetness.^h The property of the great red crown has been brought to me. The great red crown has been given to me. Cause that I may go forth on this day against my enemy, that I may carry him off, and that I may be powerful over him. THIS BOOK WAS UNDER THE FLANKS OF KHNUM.^i Thus it concludes.^j

CT 1084 (55)

B^k [355] I am the lord of blood on the days^1 of becoming. I am the sharp-one. I have not robbed. Make way for me in front of the temple. The embalmer belongs to those who are in^m sweetness 356 who brought the property of the red crown to me.

    ^a Version B occurs in B1L and B2L. Cf. BD 179b.
    ^b B1L omits shm.i im.f.
    ^c B2L has "of the Great-one (fem.)."
    ^d Version C occurs in B1Be, B5C and twice in B1P.
    ^e B1P omits the last two sentences.
    ^f Or "⌜those-of-the-knives⌝"; mdsw in B1Be and B5C, dsw in B1P.
    ^g Either the verb wt with n before its object or "I am the embalmer of" with m of predication omitted.
    ^h Barguet, Le Livre des Morts, p. 264, suggests "le vin de palme" for bnit.
    ^i Khnum is only clear on B1Be.
    ^j The colophon only occurs in B1Be.
    ^k Version B occurs in B1L twice and once each in B2L and B2P.
    ^1 B2L has "day."
    ^m B1L apparently has sw for imyw due to the slight difference in the signs involved.

Thus the short version of the Book of Two Ways (version C) ends with the deceased able to identify himself with the god Osiris who prevails over his enemies. A journey past demon gatekeepers is still the setting for these spells but Osiris is clearly regarded as the most important god here and throughout the book according to this version.

SECTION VI

Section VI can be regarded as a local tradition describing the "Beyond" with emphasis on Thoth the god of Hermopolis.

Spell 1088 consists of the names of various demons from three coffins with version A and the label "flame" on a door of three coffins with version B.

CT 1088 (59)

A   [366]"Who brings a head." "Flaming-one."[a]
"Who brings a head." "One who possesses ⌈the baboons⌉[b] of Setaw.[c]
"The living-ones." "One who possesses ⌈the baboons⌉.
"Baboon."[d]

B[e]   [366]Flame.

[a]Nsrw. These two names occur on B12C.
[b]Bnwt (?) Cf. Wb, I, 458, 6 and 464, 9-11 for bnw and bnt! "Pavian." Also possible is Wb. I, 459, 3 "der Geile."
[c]St!w probably for r-st!w. These are on B2Bo.
[d]Iꜥn. B9C has these three names.
[e]This occurs on B1L, B2L, and B2P.

The order of the next few spells is generally according to B2Bo since the ancient editor's choice seems more logical here than the modern editor's (cf. JAOS 91 [1971] 35, note 23).

Spell 1093 provides the heading for the section, "this is the way of Thoth toward the house of Maat." It adds that the deceased "will be in the suite of Thoth at night."

CT 1093 (64)

A[a] [371]This is the way of Thoth toward the house of Maat.
372 I shall be in the suite of Thoth at night towing them.[b]

B^c [371] Your way, O Thoth, is toward the house of Maat. ^{372}I shall be in the suite of Thoth at night towing it. Flame.

^{a}Version A occurs in B3C, B4C, B2Bo, B6C, and B12C. B9C has affinities to version A here and also has a partial parallel to spell 1092 in version B.

^{b}B9C adds "I am in possession of Maat; darkness is my abomination. [I see] l[ight]. (I) open darkness."

^{c}Version B occurs in B1L, B2L, and B2P.

CT 1089 is principally a recitation to Re of the deceased's accomplishments. We learn here that the bark sails on water at night and that this water is from rain. The šd wʿrt, "plots of land of the district," are comparable to the deceased's šht, "plots of land," in the sht htpw, "Field of Offerings," in spell 1048.

CT 1089 (60)

A^a ^{367}Cause that I be brought to you, O Thoth.^{b} I am the one who opens the underworld (dwꜣt).^{c} O Re, I raise your head that I may sail in^d your bark ^{368}and that I may make your way in the sky, which drips^e water on which you^f may sail at night.^{g} ^{369}I am the one who is silenced in the midst of^h a plot of land of the district.^{i} Make way for this ⌜Rod⌝^{j} and ⌜Necky⌝.^{k} Make way for me that I may repel bleariness from the All-lord,^{370}that I may spit on the wounds of Re with the result that he may live sweetly.^{l} I am the one who knows^m how to oppose^n Apopis with the result that he retreats.^{o}

B^p ^{367}I cause that I be brought to you, O bull of the constellation. O Re, I raise your head that I may sail your bark, ^{368}that I may make your way in this sky, the lord^q of your district,^{r} and that the water ⟨may go down⟩^{s} so that your bark may sail on it at night. ^{369}I am the one who is silenced in the midst of a pool of water.^{t} Make^u his way in^v flame.^{w} Make way for me, O "Rejected-of-face,"^{x} "He-of-the-Rushes,"^{y} that I may repel bleariness from the limits.^{z}

Section VI

^aVersion A occurs in B3C, B4C, B1Bo, B4Bo, B6C, B2Bo and B12C. B9C has affinities to both versions A and B.

^bB1Bo omits "Thoth" and has "Cause that this N. who opens the underworld be brought to you."

^cB3C has m [tp], "This N. rises in front of you." B6C has "your head was raised up by this N."

^dB6C and B12C omit m.

^eThis transitive meaning of ḥȝ is proposed to account for the t in B2Bo and B4Bo.

^fB4C and B9C have "your bark," and B2Bo omits k.

^gB1Bo has "The water goes down so that your bark may sail on it at night." B12C has "and that I may go down ⟨in⟩ the day bark in which you sail at night."

^hCryptic writing of m-hnw with three water-signs. The nw-jar is found only on B12C.

ⁱWꜥrt. B12C omits šd and has water determinative, "in the midst of the waters."

^jIȝȝw.

^kNhbty. B1Bo has nwḥ, "⌜rope⌝."

^lB1Bo has "Re whom this N. knew (to be) pleasant."

^mB4C ends here.

ⁿB12C omits hsf, "who knows Apopis."

^oB2Bo adds "very peacefully." B1Bo has "so that he retreats." Perhaps B12C has hfty "enemy" instead of htỉ or htỉ.f.

^pVersion B occurs in B1L, B2L, and B2P.

^qB9C has nbt, "the mistress."

^rB1L has "waters."

^sIt seems that hȝ survived in version B as ȝ.

^tŠd wꜥrt with water determinative.

^uB2P ends here.

^vB1L omits m.

^wB2L adds "I have made his way in flame," and this concludes the text.

^xNỉȝ ḥr.

^yN(y) ḥnwt(y).

^zḤr drw.

Spell 1094 is also addressed to Thoth. In this spell the deceased is a guide for both eyes of Horus, the sun and the moon. Maat is probably "order" in the lake, i.e., the sky (ECT, VII 375 c). The deceased goes down in the sun bark and saves Re, the sound eye, from Apopis without falling into his fetters.

CT 1094 (65)

A[a] [372]Hail to you, Thoth, who are in the suite of Re. [373]I am the one who brought the dazzling sound eye. I am the one who removed[b] bleariness from the injured eye that it might dazzle. [374]I have come to you in this your suite of the night among those who make offerings. I went down in the[c] bark of Re [375]after I ⌈had watered⌉[d] the flame, having lightened[e] the darkness among those who come with offerings, bringing Maat to the one who crosses the lake[f] [376]and after he had heard the speech[g] of "Confusion"[h] at the great northern district of Stretching-the-bows. I am the one who has saved Re from the raging of Apopis. [377]He has[i] not fallen into his fetters. I am the one who has made a disturbance, who has cleansed the injured eye, who has gone around the door, who has adorned the god with what he has made. [378]Cause that I be brought to you, O Thoth. I have not opposed you[j] at night. I am the one who has brought the sound eye, who has rescued it from its ⌈yellowness⌉.[k] [379]The mansion of the Moon is witness.

B[1] [372]Hail to you, Thoth, in the suite of Re. [373]I am the one who brought the sound eye that it might dazzle. [374]I have come to you in this your suite of the night among those who make offerings. I have gone down in the bark of Re [375]⌈having watered⌉ the flame that I may lighten the darkness among those who come with offerings, bringing[m] Maat to the one who crosses the lake [376]after he has heard[n] the voice of "Confusion" at the northern district of Stretching-the-bows. I am the one who has saved Re from the raging of Apopis. [377]I have not fallen into his fetters. I am the one who has rescued the sound eye, who has cleansed the injured eye, who has gone around the door, who has equipped the god with what he has made. [378]I have not opposed you, O Thoth, at night.

[a]Version A occurs in B3C, B4C, B1Bo, B2Bo, B4Bo, B6C, and B12C. B9C has affinities to both versions A and B.

[b]B1Bo has wdꜥ; all other mss. have dr. Roccati, Papiro Ieratico, p. 33 note 1, has "io ho respinto l'obnubilamento...."

[c]B3C has "your bark, O Re."

^{d}Mwy.

^{e}B6C and B12C have "flame which lightened."

^{f}"Sky" in B2Bo and B4Bo.

^{g}B6C and B12C have hrw "noise" for mdw.

^{h}Hiw with an ass-determinative, cf. CT 1041/1152 note d. B4Bo has hrw for hiw. Hornung is probably correct in associating hiw and Apopis, cf. his Amduat, III, 64. For hiw as "ass" and a name of Seth cf. Borghouts, Magical Texts, p. 144, note 344.

^{i}B2Bo has "I have."

^{j}B6C and B12C have "I shall not oppose you."

^{k}Kn. Roccati, Papiro Ieratico, p. 38 note d, has "assalitore."

^{l}Version B occurs in B1L, B2L, and B2P.

^{m}B1L has m int but B2L and B2P have m iwt (?).

^{n}B2L and B2P have sdm.f "when he hears" or "so that he may hear" for sdm.n.f. On B2P the spell ends here.

Spell 1090 is a collection of names, probably of demons, found in the plan of what seems to be the "house of Maat" named in 1093.

CT 1090 (61)

A^a [370]„⌜Necky⌝."^{b} "Contrary-face."^{c} "Possessor-of-joy." "Possessor-of-rain."   "Possessor-of-adoration."

B^d [370]„⌜Necky⌝."   Flame. Flame. Its name is "Contrary-face."   "Transgressor."^{e} "Possessor-of-adoration."

^{a}This occurs in B2Bo with two of the names also in B4C.
^{b}Nhbti.
^{c}Nhi-hr, cf. CT 1135 note c.
^{d}Version B occurs in B1L, B2L, B2P, and B9C.
^{e}Hr-iw, cf. Wb. I, 48, 9.

Spells 1091 and 1092 are found only on B-version coffins, where this house is more clearly illustrated. The spells occur on walls of flame and darkness respectively. In 1091, the deceased appears to be usurping royal prerogatives by saying that he "will not burn while wearing the nemes and the white crown." This could indicate this spell's royal and Upper Egyptian origin or association, but it occurs here in the apparently local section.

CT 1091 (62)

B[a]   [371]The flame which is around and which burns there.[b] I shall not burn while I am wearing the nemes or the white crown. The ⌜Tjennut-gods⌝[c] have come to be having come to be as Khepri.

[a]This occurs in B1L, B2L, and B2P.
[b]Zandee, Death, p. 140, translates this "Oh flame, backwards! You that burns there."
[c]Tnnw, cf. CT 1133 note b.

CT 1092 is a rubric in which Thoth is addressed by the deceased.

CT 1092 (63)

B[a]   [371]HAIL TO YOU, THOTH, WHO WAS CHOSEN AS LORD IN[b] EARLY MORNING. I AM IN POSSESSION OF MAAT. ⟨DARKNESS⟩ IS (MY) ABOMINATION. I ⌜SEE⌝[c] THE LIGHT. I OPEN THE DARKNESS.

[a]This occurs in B1L, B2L, and B2P.
[b]B2P omits m.
[c]N$.1, or, an early use of the possessive article, "MY LIGHT IS THE ABOMINATION OF DARKNESS."?

In CT 1095, the one whom Isis precedes and guides across the sky is Thoth who is named in 1096.

CT 1095 (66)

A[a]   [379]This is Isis who is before him in Maat. She shows him the ways in crossing the sky, that he may imitate what Re does.

B[b]   [379]This is Isis who is before him in Maat. She serves as guide for him of the way to cross the sky, the likeness of Re.

    [a] Version A occurs in B2Bo, B4C, B6C, and B9C.
    [b] Version B occurs in B1L, and B2L.

In spell 1096, Thoth has the "eye of Horus" before him and this is probably the bark depicted in the enclosure of 1098. "Mansion of the moon" apparently is a heading for 1098 which continues this group even though it begins the lower register on most coffins.

CT 1096 (67)

A,B[a] 380 This is Thoth who is in the sky, the eye of Horus before him in[b] the mansion of the moon.[c]

    [a] This occurs in B1L, B4C, B9C, B12C, B2L, and B2P.
    [b] B1L omits m.
    [c] B12C has only the name "Thoth" for this spell.

In CT 1097, version B designates a "possessor of joy," and also labels as "flame" the doors shown. The label "possessor of joy" occurs on the plan of B1L in the place which corresponds exactly to the place on B1C where a man is standing at the doors. This completely human figure probably represents the deceased, and the label would refer to him as well.

CT 1097 (68)

B[a] [380] "Possessor-of-joy." Flame. Flame.

    [a] These occur in B1L, B2L, and B9C.

In spell 1098 the entourage of Thoth is designated as "common folk (rhyt)" in version A and "celebrated ones (rhhywt)" in B. On both versions Thoth appears to be identified as Re who shines in the night. A stylized bark, perhaps the "coiled one," occurs in the lower of two compartments formed by three blue representations of the sky. In Amduat (12th hour, no. 778, p.185)

and in the Book of Gates (1st division, no. 5, p.28) mhn is a
serpent who surrounds the shrine of Re.

CT 1098 (69)

A[a] ^{381}As for this coiled one which is before him (Thoth), it
is Isis who[b] brought it to him. The elder Horus says:
Make his (Thoth's) name prosper on this day of their protecting against him (Apopis) there ^{382}in the horizon, when
the entourage in the horizon divides, when they bring their
great ones,[c] and when his father (Re)[d] who is among the
gods speaks. ^{383}You[e] have made the[f] entourage from your
common folk. I[g] cause that they reach you.[h] The one who
shines in the night is Re. ^{384}As for any person who is
in his suite, he lives forever[i] among the followers of
Thoth. ^{385}It is in the night that he is made to appear and
Osiris is gladdened since he is the unique one who suf-
fered[j] more than he did, after having been placed among his
followers in the[k] entourage.

B[l] ^{381}As for this coiled one,[m] this is what is before him.
It is Isis who brought it to him and (it is) Re, the great
one, the elder, who recited spells[n] for (me) to protect
them[o] against him there ^{382}in the horizon. When the entourage divided, he, namely his father who is among these,
brought away their great ones. ^{383}You (plu.) make his
entourage, which will be precious to him, as his celebrated ones. The one who shines in the night is Re.
^{384}This is the great one for whom the sky came to be. As
for any person who will be[p] in his suite, he will live in
the suite of Thoth ^{385}and he will be made to appear in
the night in the joy of Osiris. You are the son of the one
who suffers alone. His father has been given to him in
his entourage.[q]

B6C.   [a]Version A occurs in B3C, B4C, B4Bo, B2Bo, B1C[a], and
B9C has affinities to both versions.
[b]B3C and B4Bo have in instead of int.
[c]B2Bo has "bringing to him its great ones."
[d]B2Bo has wr, "the Great-one."

^{e}Mostly feminine (Isis?), but B4Bo has the masculine k, and the suffix is plural in B2Bo and B6C.

^{f}"Your" in B4Bo (masculine) and B1C^a (feminine). Apparently f "his" in B4C.

^{g}Another first person pronoun of the original was overlooked in B3C.

^{h}Generally feminine, but masculine in B4Bo. B2Bo has m before Rꜥ in the following statement, perhaps "in that day when I shine in the night."

^{i}B4Bo omits ỉw.f ꜥnh dt.

^{j}Nwd, cf. Faulkner's translation of PT 829e and 2112.

^{k}B1C^a, B6C, and B9C have "in his entourage."

^{l}Version B occurs in B1L, B2L, B3L, B1C^b, and B2P.

^{m}B3L has "this living one."

^{n}ỉr n(.ỉ) tpw-rw.

^{o}Or, "at their palace," since stp sꜣ has a house determinative.

^{p}B2L has "as for any person who knows it, he will be..."

^{q}B2L has "in his suite and entourage." B3L has "in the suite and entourage," B1C^b has "in his suite and in his entourage."

SECTION VII

Spell 1099 is the longest spell in the book and it occurs without vignette or plans. Section VII consists of this one spell but perhaps CT 1065 was a part of this originally. In 1099 the deceased recites a list of his services to Re which includes causing his image to ascend in the morning and knotting his chapel shut at night. What looks like a negative confession of the deceased is probably no more than a description of his successful navigation of the solar bark. He asks judges to estimate his importance and elaborates further on his conduct and Re's appreciation. He identifies himself with Re but also worships Re. He gives the entourage a joyful voyage while sitting or kneeling at the prow of the "eye." He opposes Apopis and since he knows the names of other evil ones, they cannot reach the bark.

CT 1099 (70)

A^a ^{386}I am a follower of Re who receives his iron, who replaces^b the god in the^c shrine, Horus who ascends to his lord. The seat was hidden ^{387}in the purification of the chapel of the messenger of the God to her whom he loved. I am the one who rescued^d Maat after he had caused his image to ascend. ^{388}I am the one who knotted the rope and bound his chapel.^{e} The storm was my abomination. There was no ⌜water-flood⌝^{f} beside me. ^{389}I have not been opposed by Re. I have not been repulsed by him who acts with his hands. I have not walked in the valley of darkness. ^{390}I have not entered into the lake of criminals. I have not been in the heat of the striking force (of God). I have not fallen as a prey ^{391}when it enters into "Faceless" and "He-who-is-around-the-slaughter-place"^{g} of the slaughter place of Sothis. Hail to you, judges. The holiness of God is ^{392}secret. The arms of Geb rise early in the morning. Who will lead the great ones and count children at his proper time? ^{393}Thoth is inside the secrets that he may make offerings to the one who counted millions and who is counted, who opened the firmament and dispelled bleariness from about him ^{394}after I^h reached him in his seat. I grasp the staff, that I may receive the Nemes ⌜rather than⌝^{i} Re, great of beautiful goings.^{j} ^{395}Horus ⌜rises⌝^{k} after his eye, his two ⌜(female) enneads⌝^{l} around^m his seat. May they repel misery and pain when he is ill. Misery has been repelled ^{396}that I may refresh the one who has it^n after I have opened the horizon for Re that his bark may make a good voyage for me ^{397}and that Thoth may be cheerful for me. I adore Re^o that he may listen to me and that he may remove an obstacle for me. I was not boatless. ^{398}I was not turned back from the horizon. I am Re. I was not boatless in^p the great crossing. It is "He-whose-face-is-on-his-knees" who extended his^q arm, ^{399}since the name of Re was in my belly and his rank was in my mouth. I say it to him^r and I am the one who hears his words. ^{400}Adoration to you,^{s} O Re, lord of the horizon. O Re, hail to you^t for whom the sun-folk purify themselves and for whom the sky acts as controller rather than the great striking force (of God) ^{401}which the courses of the rebellious^u pass. I have come^v among those who herald Maat, since the god Biau is in the west, ^{402}so that he may break the rage of Apopis and Ruty. I make known to you^w that I have come. (O you) who are before the great seat, may you listen to me ^{403}when I go down in your Council^x that I may rescue Re from Apopis every day. I have not attacked him while awake, O ⌜superintendent⌝.^{y} ^{404}I grasp the writing that I may receive the offerings, and that I may equip Thoth with what he has made. I cause Maat to go around in front of the great bark ^{405}and he who is justified to go down in the Council. I establish the millions^z that I may lead the entourage. May I give them ^{406}a voyage in sheer^{aa} joy that the crew of Re may go around after his^{ab} beauty. May Maat be high that she may reach her lord.^{ac} ^{407}Adoration is given to the All-lord that I may receive the staff and sweep the sky with it. May the sun-people give me adoration as when the unwearying one (Re) rises ^{408}that I may exalt Re by what I do for him,^{ad} that I may dispel bleariness,^{ae} that I may see his beauty, that I may cause his slaughtering,^{af} that I may set his^{ag} course, ^{409}and that his bark may go around the sky at^{ah} dawn. I am the great one in the midst of his eye,^{ai} sitting or kneeling^{aj} in front of the great^{ak} bark of Khepri.^{al} ^{410}As I come into existence so does what I say come into existence. I am that one who goes around the sky to the west. The ⌜risers⌝^{am} stand while Shu is rejoicing, ^{411}after they received the prow-rope of Re from his crew. Re goes around the sky at my bidding in peace and contentment. I have not been opposed. ^{412}The blast of your^{an} striking force has not overtaken me.^{ao} You have uttered nothing that would hinder me. I have not gone on the ways^{ap} of pestilence. ^{413}The abomination of my ka is falling from it. The flood is my abomination. It has not reached me.^{aq} I have not gone down to your^{ar} bark. His throne has been provided^{as} ^{414}that I may assume dignity and that I may lead the ways of Re and the stars. I am the one who has opposed this evil one who came to set fire to your bark ^{415}upon the Great District. I know them by their names. They did not reach your bark while I was in it. I am the one who made offerings.

B^{at} ^{386}I am a follower of Re who receives his iron, who replaces his shrine, Horus^{au} who ascends to his lord, whose seat was hidden ^{387}in the purification of his chapel, a messenger of the God to her whom he loved. I am the one who rescued Maat after he had caused his image to ascend. ^{388}I am the one who knotted the rope and bound his chapel. The storm was my abomination. There was no ⌜water-flood⌝ beside me. ^{389}I have not been opposed by Re. I have not been repulsed by him who acts with his hands. I have not walked in the valley of darkness. ^{390}I have not entered into the lake of criminals. I have not been in the heat of the striking force (of God). I have not fallen as a prey ^{391}whose soul is with "Faceless" and "He-who-is-around-the-slaughter-place" of the slaughter place of Sothis. Hail to you, Judges.^{av} The holiness of God is ^{392}secret. The arms of Geb^{aw} rise early in the morning. Who will lead the great ones and count children at his proper time?

^{393}Thoth is inside the secrets that he may make offerings to the one who counted millions, who opened the firmament and dispelled bleariness from about him, ^{394}after I reached him in his seat. I grasp the^{ax} staff that I may receive the Nemes ⌜rather than⌝ Re, great of his beautiful^{ay} goings. ^{395}Horus ⌜rises⌝^{az} after his eye, his ennead around his seat. May they repel misery and pain when he has been ill.^{ba} May I repel misery ^{386}that I may refresh the one who has it that I may open^{bb} the horizon for Re that his bark may make a good voyage for me^{397}and that Thoth may be cheerful for me. I adore Re, that he may listen to me and that he may remove an obstacle for me. I was not boatless. ^{398}I was not turned back from the horizon. I am Re. I was not boatless in the great crossing. It is the "One-whose-face-is-on-his-knees" who extended (his) arm,^{bc} ^{399}since the name of Re was in my belly and his rank in my mouth. I say it to him and I am the one who hears his words. ^{400}Adoration to you, O Re, lord of the horizon. O Re, hail to you for whom the sun-folk purified themselves and for whom the sky acts as controller rather than this great striking force of God ^{401}which the courses of the rebellious pass. I have come heralding Maat since (the god) Biau is in the west, ^{402}after he has broken the rage of Apopis and Ruty. I am the one who makes known to you that I ⟨have come⟩.^{bd} (O you) who are before the great seat, may you listen to me, ^{403}when I go down in your Council that I may rescue Re from Apopis every day. He has not attacked him so that he may awaken me. ^{404}I grasp the writing that I may receive the offerings, that I may equip Thoth with what he has done and that I may cause Maat to go around in front of the great bark ^{405}(since I) possess justification in the Council. I establish the millions that I may lead the entourage and that I may give them ^{406}a voyage in joy. Let the crew of Re^{be} go around after his beauty. May Maat be high that she may reach her lord. ^{407}Adoration is given to the All-lord that I may receive the staff and that I may sweep the sky with it. May the sun-people give me adoration as when the unwearying one rises, ^{408}that I may exalt Re by what I have done for him, that I may dispel bleariness, that I^{bf} may see his beauty, that I may cause his slaughtering, that I may set his course, ^{409}and that his bark may go around the sky at dawn. I am the great one in the midst of his eye, sitting or kneeling in the great bark of Khepri. ^{410}As I come into existence, so does what I say come into existence. I am that one who goes around the sky to the west. The ⌈risers⌉ stand while Shu is rejoicing, ^{411}after they received the prow-rope of Re from his crew. Re goes around the sky at my bidding in peace and contentment. I have not been opposed. ^{412}The blast of your striking force has not overtaken me. You have uttered nothing that would hinder me. I have not gone on the ways of pestilence. ^{413}The abomination of my ka is falling from it. Scum[bg] is my abomination. It has not reached me. I go down to your bark that I may provide your[bh] throne, ^{414}that I may assume his dignity and that I may lead the way of Re to[bi] the constellation. I am the one who has opposed this evil one who came to set fire to your bark ^{415}upon the Great District. I know them by their names. They did not reach your bark[bj] while I was in it. I am the one who made offerings.

[a]Version A occurs in B3C, B4C, B1Bo, B4Bo, B2Bo, B1C, B6C, and B12C. B9C has affinities to both versions A and B. B9C begins with Dd mdw. Cf. BD 130b.

[b]Dbꜣ, or "adorns."

[c]B3C, B4Bo, B1C, and B6C add "his."

[d]Sd, or "recited"? B1Bo has dd "who spoke."

[e]B4Bo has "his rope," and B4C and B1C have "the chapel."

[f]Wbs, cf. Allen, BD, p. 214 note k; BD has hꜣ-bꜣs, "starry host." Cf. also ECT, VII 410 c.

[g]B1Bo has hꜣ{.f} nmt. B12C has "around their slaughter place and the slaughter place of Sothis."

[h]B1Bo apparently loses control of the subject, at times using the name and correctly substituting the f-suffix, at times reverting back to an earlier first person written or unwritten.

[i]R, otherwise "against."

[j]B1C apparently has "great because of Re's beautiful goings."

[k]BD and B3L have wbn; for wbs cf. Wb.I, 296, 6-8, a late word meaning "arise" or "spring forth," with reference to plants.

[l]Dual with female determinatives, or, "his Psdty."

Section VII

^{m}"Around" is written ḥȝ sp-2.

^{n}Or, "who undergoes it;" ḥry is "him who is under it" literally.

^{o}B3C and B4C add "by acting for him."

^{p}The preposition m was omitted in mss. with version A.

^{q}Only B2Bo has f.

^{r}B12C has "he said it to me."

^{s}B1Bo omits k.

^{t}B3C omits Rꜥ ỉnd ḥr.k.

^{u}B1Bo has mntw, "Bedouin." All other mss. have sntw.

^{v}B3C ends here.

^{w}B1Bo omits this.

^{x}B4C has "in the Council of this N."

^{y}Written rwf in B1Bo and B2Bo, but either rwf or rwd in B6C and B12C.

^{z}Cf. Hornung, Amduat, III, 60.

^{aa}Tpt, cf. Allen BD, p. 215, note ao.

^{ab}B2Bo omits f.

^{ac}B2Bo omits nb.s.

^{ad}B12C has ỉr.n.ỉ n.f "what I have done for him."

^{ae}B1Bo omits ḥȝty.

^{af}Or, "terror of him." B1Bo and B2Bo omit f "his."

^{ag}B1Bo omits f.

^{ah}Written n for m in all but B1L of B-version.

^{ai}B1Bo has "in the midst of his bark, in the midst of his eye."

^{aj}B1C omits mỉs.

^{ak}B1C omits ꜥȝ.

^{al}B1Bo adds "who comes into being by himself."

^{am}B1Bo has wbw for wbsw.

^{an}B6C has "his."

^{ao}B2Bo and B6C have "He has not been overtaken by the blast of your (his) striking force."

^{ap}B2Bo has "mounds."

^{aq}For these last two statements, B6C has "The abomination of this N. has reached him."

^{ar}B12C has "his."

^{as}B12C and B9C have "that I may provide his throne."

^{at}Version B occurs in B1L, B2L, B3L, and B2P.

^{au}B9C, B2L, and B3L add dr before Ḥr, "until Horus ascends"?

^{av}B3L has "Gods and Judges."

[aw] B1L omits "Geb."
[ax] B2L has "his."
[ay] B1L omits nfr(w)t.
[az] B3L has wbn; B1L and B2L have wbs.
[ba] B1L has "Misery and pain were dispelled whenever he had been ill."
[bb] B1L has "after I have opened."
[bc] B1L has the dual "arms."
[bd] Version B has only mk wỉ omitting ỉỉ.kwỉ.
[be] B1L omits "of Re."
[bf] B2L and B3L have "he."
[bg] ṯhw, cf. Wb. I, 12, 15, and Allen, BD, p. 215, note az.
[bh] B2L has "his."
[bi] Omitted in B2L and B3L; r is questionable in B1L. Perhaps "and" as in the A-version.
[bj] B1L adds "while I was ⟨in⟩ your bark."

SECTION VIII

Seven gatekeepers occur in section VIII in two groups. In the first group, four keepers occur one behind the other. Spell 1100 presents the first of these keepers, and the deceased boasts before it.

CT 1100 (71)

A,B[a] 416"THE ONE WHO STRETCHES OUT[b] THE PROW-ROPE,"[c] THE KEEPER OF THE OUTSIDE[d] GATE.[e] I came here from the great valley after I had taken the ⌜knives⌝[f] of the ⌜knife fighter⌝[g] from him. 417The Butcher,[h] sharp of the striking force (of god),[i] which has no opposition. I am the one who opposes the Evil-ones[j] which have no opposition. Do not charge down upon me.[k] 418O you who stretch out the prow-rope,[l] "Watchful-face," let there not be bleariness[m] in the sun people on the day of the holiness of God. If you come against me[n] 419with every kind of[o] worm, then Re will die, and Apopis will be slaughtered. Things were done[p] in accordance with him in the midst of the slaughter place of the protector.[q]

[a]Version A occurs in B3C, B4C, B1Bo, B2Bo, B1C, B6C, B12C, and B9C. Version B occurs in B1L, B3L, and B2P.

[b]B3L omits d of dwn.

[c]Ḥȝt for ḥȝtt, cf. B12C in ECT, VII 418 a. The keeper of the second door in BD 144 has this same name. Cf. Allen BD, p. 232, note c, "⌜Spy⌝" is his translation.

[d]Ḥȝt; or is it "first," a writing of ḥȝwty?

[e]The entire heading was omitted in B1Bo, B2Bo, B6C, and B12C, and it was not rubricized in B4C or B9C.

[f]Taking srtyw with knife determinative as "⌜knives⌝." Srtyw could also be "sheep." B3C has shtyw for srtyw, "⌜strikers⌝"? and B12C has sȝṯ for sȝṯty? "mutilator."

[g]ꜥḥȝ with knife and divine determinative.

[h]Sšm?

[i]B4C, B9C, B1L, B3L and probably B2P omit ȝt.

^{j}B1Bo has sn bwt "them, the abominated," B4C omitted N tn hsf before nbdw.

^{k}Written as first person in B3C also.

^{l}Written ẖṯtt only in B12C, otherwise ẖṯt.

^{m}Hpr.f ẖṯty in all but B9C which omits f.

^{n}Only B9C, B1L, and B3L have r.ỉ.

^{o}B9C, B1L, and B3L omit nbt.

^{p}Or, "Offerings were made."

^{q}B4C, B9C, B1L, and B3L add "by the one who destroyed his father."

The keeper of the second gate in spell 1101 is apparently misnamed on B3C since this ms. has the name of the keeper which is at the last gate (ECT, VII 439 a) in the other mss. The name in the A-version of 1101 should probably be the same as that in version B. The protecting Uraeus is again reminiscent of royal texts.

CT 1101 (72)

A,B^a ^{420}"THE ONE WHO CUTS THEM DOWN," THE KEEPER OF THE SECOND GATE.^{b} May you avoid the one who acts perversely toward you.^{c} My Uraeus has protected me. ^{421}"Confusion" was standing opposite you. The bark^d is fallen upon the ⌜rough⌝^{e} water. You ⌜pour out that which is⌝^{f} in the mouth of Re. ^{422}You have not travelled^g with his^h suite. The striking force (of God) is before you,^{i} his tongue^j against you. Retreat from your seat. You have not come (in) his time.^{k} You are seen,^{l} ^{423}O aggressor who is below, because^m the Great-one^n comes.

^{a}Version A occurs in B3C, B4C, B1Bo, B2Bo, B1C, B6C, and B12C. Version B occurs in B1L, B3L, B2P, and B9C.

^{b}B3C has "⌜IKENTY⌝" cf. ECT, VII 439 a. The name is completely lost in B4C and B1C, and omitted in the rest of the mss. with Version A.

^{c}For nwd r cf. also ECT, VII 385 c. This statement occurs in B4C and the B-version mss.

^{d}B2Bo has "the bark of Re." B12C has "you are in the bark which has fallen..."

^{e}Gnn usually means "weak." Version B has "flood-water."

Section VIII

^f Reading i̓w.k (hr) s(ꜣ)t ntf.

^g B3C has wdỉ, "You have not been healthy," but B2Bo, B1C, B6C, B12C, and version B have dỉ.

^h B9C, B3L, and B2P omit f.

^i B4C and B1Bo omit k and, together with version B, could be "the striking force of Ḥernetjef is against you," cf. ECT, VII 435 c. B2P ends in the middle of this name.

^j Nt, cf. PT, 1088c.

^k Or, "that he may be excluded"?. B9C has "He has not come" probably omitting k sp by haplography.

^l B6C ends here. B1L has "You have not been seen."

^m B9C, B1L, and B3L omit n.

^n Feminine, the "Eye (bark)"?

The third gatekeeper in CT 1102 is also the keeper of the third gate in BD 147c. Since the deceased knows him and the name of his throwstick, light goes forth to open the firmament.

CT 1102 (73)

A,B^a [423] THE ONE WHO EATS THE EXCREMENT OF HIS REAR, THE KEEPER OF THE THIRD GATE.^b Turn back, ^424 aggressor, your arm is as the ⌜abeḥu-plants⌝.^c Your back is as the red bebet-herb. May you eat, eating the ⌜memet-plant⌝.^d ^425 I know you.^e I know the name of this your throwstick which was thrown behind you.^f On your face! Let your arms go down ^426 that light may go forth, that it may open the^g firmament, and that bleariness of face may dispel it.^h

^a Version A occurs in B3C, B4C, B1Bo, B2Bo, B1C, and B6C. Version B occurs in B1L, B3L, B2P, and B9C.

^b Cf. BD 147c. The heading was omitted in B1Bo, B2Bo, and B6C.

^c ꜣbhw, perhaps related to bh, cf. Wb. I, 468, 6.

^d Cf. PT 1362b, and Sethe's Kommentar.

^e B1Bo has "which he throws."

^f Version B has "which you have thrown behind yourself."

^g B2Bo, B6C, and B9C have "its" or "his."

^h Version B can be translated "may be dispelled."

The fourth gatekeeper in CT 1103 (likewise the keeper named in BD 147d) also submits.

CT 1103 (74)

A,B[a] [426] OPPOSED-FACE, NOISY, THE KEEPER OF THE FOURTH GATE.[b] 427 Shu and Ruty, Shu[c] to the sky, Ruty to earth. It is you who say to me: Holy is the sky and the earth. On your face! The white crown and the nemes have retreated.[d] 428 He enters[e] after "Opposed-face"[f] trembled[g] around the holiness of God which reached ⌈asret⌉.[h] Who is it that goes around[i] the Coiled-one, 429 great of dignity?[j] Let Thoth decide in early morning.[k] The bark has been broken up since you[l] have come opposed to me.

[a] Version A occurs in B3C, B4C, B1Bo, B2Bo, B1C, and B6C. Version B occurs in B1L, B3L, and B2P. B9C has affinities to both versions A and B. Cf. BD 147d.
[b] The heading is omitted in B1Bo, B2Bo, and B6C.
[c] "Shu" is omitted here in B6C, and in B3L.
[d] B3C omits nms. B1Bo repeats hm "The white crown has retreated and the nemes has retreated."
[e] Causative sʿk in A-version.
[f] B4C, B2Bo, and B6C have "this Opposed-face."
[g] Causative ssdȝ in all but B1Bo. B9C has f instead of n after ssdȝ probably in error, or "he makes Opposed-face tremble."
[h] Written ȝsrt with sky-determinative. Version B has ȝrt and ȝry, but this is certainly not the same word as in ECT, VII 327 a and 516 a.
[i] B1Bo, B2Bo, and B1L are future tense.
[j] B3C has "his dignity."
[k] B2P concludes with "having been judged."
[l] B9C omits k.

Section VIII

The next few spells are placed between the two groups of gatekeepers. In spell 1104 it is the solar Horus who goes around the sky and sees the deceased at the oars of his bark.

CT 1104 (75)

A,B[a] ⁴³⁰I have come rejoicing that I may reach[b] the number of cubits[c] of Re as[d] Khepri. (As for) Horus, the eldest[e] son of Re, he goes around[f] the sky. ⁴³¹He sees[g] me among those who are at the oars.[h]

[a]Version A occurs in B3C, B4C, B2Bo, B1Bo, B1C, and B6C. Version B occurs in B1L, B3L, B2P, and B9C.
[b]$\underline{Sr}$, or "foretell."
[c]B1Bo has $\underline{hʿw}$, "appearances," for $\underline{mhw}$.
[d]$\underline{M}$, or "with."
[e]Written $\underline{wr}$ in B1L.
[f]B2Bo and B6C add "in."
[g]B-version has "that he may see."
[h]B9C omitted "Horus, the eldest son of Re," previously and added it here.

In CT 1105 the deceased says that he preserved Maat (order) and he pursues the great crown of Horus, the eldest son of Re.

CT 1105 (76).

A,B[a] [431]I came from the sky[b] of Ruty, ⁴³²after I had preserved Maat. Make way for me that I may receive the great crown[c] (which is)[d] upon Horus, the eldest son of Re, from her and myself. Bring it to me. ⁴³³Make way for me[e] that I may pass by on it,[f] that I[e] may correct the ⌈opponent⌉,[g] and that I[e] may open darkness.

[a]Version A occurs in B3C, B4C, B2Bo, B1C, and B6C. Version B occurs in B1L, B3L, B2P, and B9C.
[b]B3C omits $\underline{m\ pt}$ and B3L has $\underline{m\ htp}$.
[c]B3C, B4C, B1L, B3L, and B2P have "receive it, (i.e.) the great crown."

114   *The Ancient Egyptian Book of Two Ways*

        ᵈOnly B3C has tpt, other mss. have tp.
        ᵉThe first person of the original was retained here on B3C.
        ᶠB3C and B2Bo omit im (B9C, B1L, B3L, and B2P) or im.s (B4C and B1C).
        ᵍVersion B has tp-mꜣ⸗t. B3C has "Maat," and B2Bo omits the object.

    The deceased comes to this Horus to be rescued in spell 1106. Again he asks that he may pass by and open the darkness.

CT 1106 (77)

A,Bᵃ [433]I have come to you, ⁴³⁴O Horus,ᵇ the eldest among the openers of the firmament, that you may rescue me from the claws of him who takes for himself what he sees.ᶜ ⁴³⁵The blast of his mouth has not taken me. His striking force has not opposed me. I have been draggedᵈ because ofᵉ ⌜Ḥernetjef⌝.ᶠ Let me pass by that I may open the darkness.ᵍ

        ᵃThis occurs in B3C, B4C, B2Bo, B1C, B6C, B9C, B1L, B3L, and B2P.
        ᵇB3C has "O Great-one."
        ᶜCf. Zandee, Death, pp. 89 and 185, for his translation of part of this spell.
        ᵈThe spell ends here on B1C.
        ᵉB9C and B1L omit hr. It could also be "on" or "from" or even "by." For some possible examples of hr = "by" cf. Borghouts, Magical Texts, p. 70 note 104.
        ᶠOr, "He who is on his tongue," cf. ECT, VII 422b.
        ᵍB3C omits kkw. B9C adds "Cause that N. pass by ⌜. . .⌝."

    Spell 1107 has the labels for darkness and its gate and also the labels on the three flaming doors of the second group of gatekeepers who appear one below the other.

CT 1107 (78)

A,B ⁴³⁶DARKNESS. DARKNESS. DARKNESS.ᵃ GATE OF DARKNESS.ᵇ Flame. Flame. Flame.ᶜ

Section VIII

[a] These headings occur in B3C, B4C, B6C, B9C, B1L, B3L, and B2P. Only B1L and B3L are rubricized.
[b] This heading occurs only in B1L.
[c] B1C, B6C, B1L, B3L and B2P have these labels.

Spell 1108 names the first in this group of gatekeepers. It is one who lives on those who do not know how to pass.

CT 1108 (79)

A,B[a] [436] UPSIDE-DOWN[b]-FACE, NUMEROUS-OF-FORMS, THE KEEPER OF THE FIRST GATE. It lives[c] on the demolishers [437] who do not know how to pass it.[d] This which is before him[e] is the spell for passing it. My protection is from him.[f] I know the crossing of "Him-who-helped-himself."[g]

[a] This occurs in B3C, B2Bo, B1C, B9C, B1L, and B3L.
[b] B3C and B1L have shd. B2Bo has shd. B9C has sdd. B3L has shr "OVERTHROWN."
[c] B1L and B3L have "who lives."
[d] B2Bo and B3L have "them."
[e] B3C has no suffix "me (?)." B2Bo has "N."
[f] B1L omits suffix "from myself." B3L has m-f.1 for the same.
[g] B2Bo adds "Invocation offerings to the revered N."

The keeper of the middle gate in CT 1109 lives on the one who does not know how to go to the sky of the elder Horus.

CT 1109 (80)

A,B[a] [437] ONE-WHO-LIVES-ON-WORMS, THE KEEPER OF THE MIDDLE GATE. He lives on the one who does not know how to go[b] to [438] this sky of the elder Horus, the third, who ascends to his lord that he may live.[c] As for what becomes worms,[d] he eats it since he[e] does not know that this which is before it is the spell for passing it. My protection is from him. I am in the midst of his firmament.[f] He is my brother,[g] the coiled one, in sailing. I am in his suite.[h]

[a] Version A occurs in B3C and B4C. Version B occurs in B1L and B3L. B1C and B9C have affinities to both versions A and B.

[b] "The spell for going" in B9C, B1L and B3L.

[c] "The third..." occurs on only B3C and B4C.

[d] B1C has "If he becomes worms." B3L has ir written with the eye-sign.

[e] B1L and B3L omit f, "I"?

[f] B3C omits hr(y)-ib. B3L has "in the midst of his bark."

[g] B-version has "He is the one who feeds you for me."

[h] B3C omits this last statement.

The keeper of the last gate in this section is named in CT 1110. The protection of the deceased in all three of these spells is said to be "from him," probably referring to the elder Horus.

CT 1110 (81)

A,B[a] 439 IKENTY,[b] WHO RAISES HIS[c] VOICE IN FLAME, THE KEEPER OF THE THIRD GATE.[d] The third[e] who ascends to his lord that he may live[f] on flame. Flame is that which is on its mouth.[g] That which is before it is the spell for passing it. My protection is from him. I am[h] in the midst of his firmament[i] with the elder Horus. 440 I cannot be attacked by ⌈those living⌉[j] or those having passed away. It is his entourage which has given prosperity to me.

[a] This occurs in B3C, B4C, B1C, B9C, B1L, B3L, and B2P.

[b] Cf. PT 433a and b for a serpent named Iken. Cf. also Allen, BD, p. 241 note an and p. 248 note x, for other occurences of the name, Ikenty. The name could be translated "⌈He-of-the-hole⌉" based on Borghouts, Magical Texts, p. 101 note 184.

[c] F is written only in B9C and B1L.

[d] B1L concludes the title with "FLAME," and omits the last phrase. Cf. Zandee, Death, p. 140, for his translation.

[e] B2P has hmt-nw only once.

[f] B2P omits f, "his lord who lives on flame."

[g] R, or "door."

[h] B4C, B1C, and B9C have "I am the lord who is in the midst...."

^{i}B3L has "bark."
^{j}Written ʿnḥ alphabetically without the ankh-sign. B9C and perhaps B1L have ḥn.

A long "flaming" door and a gate of darkness are found on most coffins after the gatekeepers, but these are labeled on only two B-version coffins in CT 1111.

CT 1111 (82)

B^a [440]$_{Flame.}$ GATE OF DARKNESS.

^{a}These occur on B1L and B3L.

In CT 1112 the deceased identifies himself with one of the gods who support the sky and announce the coming of the solar bark.

CT 1112 (83)

A,B^a [440]$_{Open}$ yourself,^{b} O Storm ^{441}that blots out^c Re, who is clothed every day when the good^d Horus^e departs.^{f} O great-form, heavy of striking force, who dispels bleariness^g by his blast,^{h} ^{442}I have come sailing, O Re. I am one of these four^i gods who are at the side of the sky, so that I may announce^j the sentry^k to you. ^{443}There is joy at your tow rope.^{l} There is no opposing you.

^{a}Version A occurs in B3C, B4C and B1Bo. Version B occurs in B1L, B3L, and B2P. B1C and B9C have affinities to both versions A and B. Cf. BD 135.
^{b}B1Bo has "Make haste." B9C, B1L and probably B1C have "I open you," while B3L has "Open to me."
^{c}Ḥꜣty (cf. Wb. III, 35, 8-12), a pun on hꜣty "storm."
^{d}B1C omits nfr.
^{e}B1Bo has a second ꜣ for the falcon.
^{f}Or "dies"? B1C has swḏꜣ for sḏꜣ, "who clothes and preserves Horus beautifully every day."
^{g}Or "cloudiness."
^{h}B9C has "from him who is in the middle." B1L and B3L have "from him who is on his face."

^{i}B3C and B4C omit "four."

^{j}B9C has "after I announced."

^{k}B1L has "sentries."

^{l}B3C and B4C have hny (cf. ECT, VII 257 b) for "joy." Other mss. with hy can be translated "O you who are towed by your rope" (cf. Wb. II, 483, 19). B1Bo seems to have "your rope goes down," cf. Allen, BD, p. 220, note g.

In spell 1113 the deceased is credited with power to heal the wounds inflicted by Apopis.

CT 1113 (84)

A,B^a [443] You have been raised on high so that I may ascend to you.^{b} Indeed you have been raised on high.^{c} 444 I am the abomination of Apopis since I know^d how to spit^e on wounds.^{f} I see, for I am the one who spits^g on the wounds so that they are well. 445 I have not opposed you, O Re.^{h}

^{a}Version A occurs in B3C, B4C, B1Bo, B1C, and B9C. Version B occurs in B1L, B2P, and B3L.

^{b}B1Bo adds "and that you may go forth." B9C begins with the following.

^{c}B4C, B1Bo, B1C, and B1L omit n, "so that you may indeed become high."

^{d}B1Bo and B1C have rh.n.i.

^{e}Version B omits psg.

^{f}B1Bo adds "your." B3L adds "my."

^{g}Without ink, B3C and B1C can be translated either "I see for I spit" or "I see the spitting."

^{h}B3C omits k "I have not opposed Re," but the scribe of B4C probably started to write k.

CT 1114 ends section VIII. No vignette accompanies the spell on any of the coffins, but the heading seems to indicate that a picture would have accompanied this on an earlier source. It is apparently the "elder Horus" with whom the deceased who knows this spell (and the whole section) will exist.

Section VIII

CT 1114 (85)

A,B^a [445] This is the elder Horus who is in this sky, the lord of every sky.^b As for any person who knows this spell which is in front of Great-form, he shall exist there as Great-form.^c Hail to you, O Re, whose beauty I see. 446 You^d have not^e attacked the evil one, your companion.

^aThis occurs in BeC, B4C, B1Bo, B1C, B9C, B1L, and B3L.

^bB3C and B4C have "who is in the ⌜united (twt)⌝ sky, (which is) the mistress of every sky." B1Bo has "who is in this sky, the mistress of the sky." B9C has "who is in this sky." B1L has "who is in every sky." B1C has "who is in every sky of the sky."

^cB1C omits the main clause here and B9C omits the whole sentence except for "as Great-form."

^dIf B3C actually had ṯ for k, it was probably a mistaken attempt to adapt the texts for Satḥedjḥetep.

^eB9C omits the negative.

SECTION IX

Spell 1115 introduces the concluding section of the Book. It labels and describes the scene which accompanies CT 1116. There are three vignettes in this last section and each illustrates a different bark. The vignettes are related to the traditions of the earlier sections and the reason for resuming them here soon becomes clear.

CT 1115 (86)

A,B^a [446]This is the drinking place of the canopy^b of God's shrine. It endures in the sky. Its front is flame, its back is darkness.

^{a}This occurs in B3C, B4C, B1C, B9C, B1L, B3L, and B2P.
^{b}Pt, or "sky."

Spell 1116 apparently contradicts 1109 by saying that the deceased will be a god even though he "does not know how to go forth to this sky of Re-Horus, the elder." From the symbolic sky with enclosed disk, similar to those found with spell 1098, and from statements related to ideas expressed in Section VI, this is evidently the goal of the section which emphasized Thoth. The deceased can live here forever, probably as a star in the sky, but he cannot join the sun-god since he does not know how to go further, presumably because he would not know the spells to enable him to do so.

CT 1116 (87)

A^a 447The one who is carrying her (Hathor's ?) ⌜jar⌝^{b} of ⌜the best⌝,^{c} the ⌜sistrum-player⌝.^{d} This is the place of a spirit who knows how to enter into flame and to open darkness, but who does not know how to go up to this sky of Re-Horus, the elder, among the followers of Re-Horus, the

120

elder, with the offerings from the horizon of Re-Horus, the elder. This is the true mystery[e] of Re. [448]Place of a very truly perfect spirit who can never die. No god ever knew one superior to him.[f] The place of a perfect spirit who shall be a god himself.

B[g] [447]The one who is carrying the jar of the Golden-one (Hathor), the ⌈sistrum-player⌉.[h] [The one who knows how to enter into] flame, who opens darkness, [but who does not know] how to go up to[i] the sky of Re among the followers of Re-Horus, the elder, in the Horizon of Re-Horus.

    [a]Version A occurs in B3C, B4C, B1C, and B9C.
    [b]Possibly bis as in B-version.
    [c]Tpw.
    [d]Written hhhh for ihy? B9C has yhhi.
    [e]ʿftt.
    [f]B4C and B9C omit this statement. For n wnt ntr nb rh.f cf. Gardiner, Grammar, §188,2. I have taken hit.f as "one superior to him," otherwise "his front."
    [g]Version B occurs in B1L, B3L, and B2P.
    [h]Or "O sistrum player." B3L has only this label.
    [i]B1L has hr for rh. This and the verbs that follow are probably imperatives "Fall into flame, open darkness, go up to the sky...."

Spell 1117 introduces a group (1117-1124) concerned with Osiris as an end. It is a spell by which the deceased will be more glorious than Osiris. This group apparently resumes Section V. CT 1117 is also closely connected to spell 1116 so that while the earlier sections may have been quite separate compositions originally, this last section which resumes them also connects them. The reference to the deceased as a "great man" in spell 1117 is perhaps significant with relation to the deceased who attains the previous and subsequent goals. Spell 1098 in Section VI referred to the entourage of Thoth as his "common-folk," and the one who could guide the solar bark or who became Re in the earlier Pyramid Texts was the deceased king, of course.

CT 1117 (88)

A,B^a [448] As for any person who knows ⌜what is sealed⌝,^{b} he is more glorious thereby than Osiris. ^{449}He has passed^c every tribunal^d in which^e Thoth is, but Thoth will be in the^f tribunal of Osiris. If a man, a great one,^{g} one who is On His Lake,^{h} is subject to going away to the beautiful^i west, it is four times that a man reads it at the purification of (that) person,^{j} and it is on his^k fourth day that he goes away, ^{450}being exact in regard to everything. But if a person^l desires to know how to cause (him) to live upon his feet,^{m} it is every day^n that he reads it, after he has rubbed his flesh with ⌜...⌝^{o} of a girl and ⌜...⌝^{p} of a bald male.^{q}

^{a}Version A occurs in B3C, B4C, and B1C. Version B occurs in B1L and B3L. B9C has affinities to both versions A and B.

^{b}Ssd_it; or, less likely, "⌜what is caused to depart⌝." Zandee, Death, p. 259, has proposed "protecting spell." B3L has sd_it "who knows how to travel."

^{c}"He passes" in B-version.

^{d}B9C has "the tribunal of the lords."

^{e}>Im.s was omitted in B3C.

^{f}B3L has "this."

^{g}B9C omitted wr. B4C has "Osiris N."

^{h}"Harsaphes"?

^{i}B1C omitted nfrt "beautiful."

^{j}Perhaps B9C and B1L add another "four times."

^{k}B9C omitted f, and with B1L and B3L probably has "fourth of four days."

^{l}B3C and B1C have "he." B4C has "any person."

^{m}B3C and B1C omit "upon his feet." B9C has "to know it in order to live upon his two feet." The scribe of B3L apparently misplaced ir and omitted rh.

^{n}B9C omitted r' nb.

^{o}Written b_id in B3C and B9C, or B_id in B1L and B3L. Possibly related to the unknown bd..t in medical texts, cf. WAD p. 188.

^{p}Written šnft. Cf. WMT, p. 862, "Krankheitsstoff." B4C has nšf....

^{q}B1C and B1L add the colophon, iw.s pw, "It means it comes" or "The end."

Spell 1118 seems to label the two water-surrounded compartments of the group, but, if so, the order should probably be reversed since Seth is mentioned only in the upper part.

CT 1118 (89)

A,B^a ^{451}Osiris-mansion, the land of (four) spirits. Seth of the land of (four) spirits.^{b}

^{a}This occurs in B3C, B4C, B1C, B9C, B1L, and B3L.
^{b}This second label was omitted in B4C.

Osiris is addressed in spell 1119.

CT 1119 (90)

A,B^a [451]He is the announcer^b of Osiris. Water^c is around him. Life is on his mouth.^{d} Assuredly, as for Osiris who has acted in the field,^{e} his two arms ⌜open⌝^{f} to him, Seth,^{g} while every^h limb in him is ^{452}in the place which it^i reached. May his limbs be splendid which he allots to^j his ⌜assemblage⌝.^{k} Hail to you, Osiris, possessor of your mansions, hidden,^{l} the weary-one,^{m} Evil-of-heart.^{n} You are stout-hearted, not fighting, but driving off uproar. I speak of the condition^o of the red^p ⌜chest⌝^{q} of the sharp-one.^{r} Count me for yourself, O Osiris. Count yourself for me,^{s} that my bones may be sound, and my limbs firm.

^{a}Version A occurs in B3C and B4C. Version B occurs in B1L and B3L. B9C has affinities to both versions A and B. Cf. Kees, OLZ, 1962, col. 591, for his translation of this spell.
^{b}S̲ỉw, or "accuser." The heading could also be "The announcer is Osiris."
^{c}B1L and B3L have "you (plu.) are around him" but tn is apparently a corruption from mw.
^{d}B9C has "that he may live in it." B3L has ḥr ry.f(y) "on his lips."
^{e}B3L has "fields."
^{f}Written sỉḥ in B3C and sỉš in B9C and B3L. Kees rendered this "absichelte." Cf. PT 712b for sỉš pertaining to ears which Sethe took as "opened" and Faulkner translates as "unstopped."

            ᵍS\]h Ꜥwy.fy n.f Stš. Kees took Seth as subject, thereby reversing the regular word order completely.
            ʰB9C omits nb.
            ⁱB3L has "they."
            ʲB-version has "when he counts" and B9C has the same with an n following.
            ᵏStwt, but B9C has stwtn.f and B-version has stwtn.
            ˡB9C seems to have "which the weary-one, Evil-of-heart, hides."
            ᵐB3L has wr ỉb "insolent-one" for wrd ỉb.
            ⁿNbd ỉb, or, perhaps "sad" as dw ỉb.
            ᵒB9C has rht "knowledge" for hrt.
            ᵖB9C and B3L apparently confuse this with r-ꜣw "entire."
            ᑫS\]\]t with a box and wood determinatives. B3C has sỉrt "need" or "wisdom."
            ʳB3C has "spiteful-one."
            ˢB3C omits "for me."

Spell 1120 is apparently a ritual to be observed. It is perhaps most important for its treatment of the ba as a soul which is breathed in.

CT 1120 (91)

A,Bᵃ ⁴⁵³I stand with Osiris when he stands. O Osiris, yourᵇ Ba comes to you.ᵇ Open yourᵇ throat. Take Osiris to Osirisᶜ (four times). The sweet winds comeᵈ to you. His striking force has been brushed aside,ᵉ after they abandoned raging on account of him forever.ᶠ

ᵃVersion A occurs in B3C, B4C, and B1C. B9C has affinities to both versions A and B. Version B occurs in B1L and B3L.
ᵇB4C has t feminine.
ᶜB9C and B1L omit "to Osiris."
ᵈB1L has "The sweet winds have come," and B3L has "have been brought."
ᵉW\]h r t\]; B4C has "after he has brushed aside his striking force."
ᶠB-version has ỉtꜤ for bt, "after they ⌜seized⌝ the one who rages."

Section IX

CT 1122 seems to continue 1120. These occur beside one another above the bark while 1121 is below. The Horus-eye is apparently used as a symbol of offering at the end of 1122 where wdȝt "sound-eye" in version A is paralleled by htpw "offerings" in version B.

CT 1122 (93)

A,B[a] [454] He does not know Seth and Osiris. Stand that I may raise you. Open your ears. The sound-eye has been given to you.[b]

[a] Version A occurs in B3C and B9C. Version B occurs in B1L and B3L.
[b] Version B has "Offerings have been given to you."

The name of the bark of Osiris is given in CT 1121 and Osiris himself is labeled on two coffins. On B1C the god is depicted in the shrine on a bark. "Aker" probably refers to the human heads at the ends of the bark.

CT 1121 (92)

A,B[a] [453] Centipede. Osiris.[b] Aker 454 Enduring and living is the name of this bark.[c]

[a] Parts of this spell occur in B3C, B4C, B6C, B1C, B9C, and B3L.
[b] "Osiris" occurs on B9C and is the only part of this spell on B6C.
[c] For this spell, B3L has only "Enduring is the name of this bark."

CT 1123 also uses "eye of Horus" (irt Hr) to symbolize offering.

CT 1123 (94)

A[a] [454] I am the one who went forth from you. Give the "eye of Horus" to Osiris. Your eye has been purified. Arise that you may live. I was satisfied after I had given.

^{a}This occurs in B3C, B1C, and B4C.

In spell 1124 the deceased in his sarcophagus (db̩t) claims to be Thoth who offers to Osiris, his father.

CT 1124 (95)

A,B^a ^{455}Being pure^b in my own sarcophagus.^{c} I am Thoth. The offerings for Osiris every day^d are my offerings. These^e belong to my father, Osiris, who is on the hill. Osiris, Aker,^{f} and the coiled one.

^{a}Version A occurs in B3C and B4C. B1C and B9C have affinities to both versions A and B. B1L and a largely illegible B3L represent version B.
^{b}B9C has "I am pure."
^{c}B1L and B3L have "My own sarcophagus has been purified.."
^{d}B3C omits rꜥ, the two nb signs after "Thoth" and "Osiris" could be taken as "lord" in apposition to the divine names.
^{e}B3C omits nn.
^{f}B3C omits "Osiris" and "Aker" and the latter is also omitted by B1C.

Spell 1125 introduces the third and last group in this section, and this group concerns the goal of the deceased according to the solar tradition. In this spell the deceased hails the portals which can rescue him on the way to the All-lord, Re, and he is evidently also involved in the contendings of Horus and Seth.

CT 1125 (96)

A,B^a [455]Hail to you, portals, hidden of names, sacred of places.^{b} ^{456}May you rescue me from every evil obstacle^c of the powerful ones who are in your presence, until I come into the presence of the All-lord. I made the two warriors content. I caused the orphan to ascend that he might cry out about the injury which^d was done against his father by ⌜Tebeh⌝ (Seth)^e who destroyed his limbs.

Section IX   127

^aThis occurs in B3C, B4C, B1C, B9C, and B1L.
^bCf. Zandee, Death, pp. 29 and 122, for his translation of much of this spell.
^cMost mss. have hw sdb "the one who implanted every evil obstacle." B4C omits hw. B1C adds "against me."
^dB1L and B9C omit nkn and read "about what was done."
^eWritten tbhi, tbhw, and tbhw, a name of Seth, cf. Tbh in Wb. V, 262, 7; and JEA, XXII, 133.

Spell 1126 names and in B1C has pictures of Apopis and his opponents, principally the four sons of Horus. The spell also labels the sun-people and crew of Re who tow the solar bark of spell 1128.

CT 1126 (97)

A[a]   457Apopis. His spine.[b] Imesty. Hapy. Daumutef. Khebeksenuef. He who sees his[c] father. He who made his own name.[d] The sun-people. The crew of Re whose number is not known.

^aThis occurs in B3C, B4C, B1C, and B9C.
^bB9C omitted "Apopis" and repeated ts.f.
^cB9C has f.
^dIr rn.f or irr n.f "He who helps himself."

CT 1127 briefly describes what the opponents of Apopis do to him.

CT 1127 (98)

A[a]   [457]Words spoken by the elder Magic. Will you travel? He will be seen fallen before thee.[b] The bowmen shoot him.[c] The spearmen make him fall.

^aThis occurs in B3C, B4C, and B9C.
^bB9C has "You will be seen fallen before her."
^cB9C has wit for pdt due to the scribe's confusing the two similar signs. The i beginning this statement in all three mss. is apparently for the particle iw.

The entourage of flame is named in CT 1128. The gods who are on the prow of the solar bark include Isis, Seth, and Horus, and, on the stern, Hu, Sia, and Re. Amduat and the Book of Gates have Sia on the front and Amduat has Seth and Horus on the back.

CT 1128 (99)

A,B[a] 458 The entourage of flame. The entourage of flame. The entourage of flame.[b] The entourage which is on the prow: Isis, Seth, and Horus. The entourage which is on the stern: Authoritative-utterance, Perception, and Re.

[a] Parts of this occur on B3C, B9C, B1L, B3L, and B1C.
[b] These labels are omitted on B3C and B9C. B1C adds "Flame ⌜which is safe⌝."

CT 1129 occurs above the bark and describes the end of its journey. The sky is described as a lake or canal with a million cubits around it in flame. When the bark lands in the west the portals again seal on it as the egg from which it came forth in the morning.

CT 1129 (100)

A,B[a] [458] Arriving at the north[b] of the ⌜winding⌝ canal,[c] the number of (whose) cities is not known. 459 A million cubits are around it (repeat) in the flame of a torch.[d] Hail to you, protectress of its blast, whom its flame made far from it. May you[e] rescue me from the one who implants[f] every evil obstacle for it, whose name[g] is "Secret-of-his-perception." I have come to be from his flesh. He[h] has created me[i] with his limbs. My father has not placed me over the one 460 from whose body[j] I cannot go forth. It lifts up my name to the rays[k] of its face. My limbs have been distinguished from my heart and from what is beautiful in my sight.[l] This[m] portal has fastened on me as the ⌜shell⌝[n] of this egg from which I had fled. It is the darkness of my father, Nun, which makes it, but this portal is far from me 461 for I have made millions of cubits into

Section IX

my own cubit in making this my place distant.

^aVersion A occurs in B3C and B4C. B9C has affinities to both versions A and B. Version B occurs in B1L and B3L.

^bB3C and probably B4C have spt for spr "the northern bank."

^cMr nḫ₃, or "lake of the lotus."

^dB1L omits tk₃.

^eB9C has t̄ and B3C has ṯ. B4C and B1L are apparently imperative.

^fB9C omits hw.

^gOnly B3C and probably B4C had rn.f.

^hB1L has s "it."

ⁱWritten i for wi in B9C.

^jB1L omits hʿw, "from whom."

^kB9C has tm (?) for stwt.

^lVersion B has "It distinguishes my limbs from my heart, it being beautiful in my sight."

^mB9C adds i, "my."

ⁿHʿw "body." See spell 1058 for another reference to the egg.

CT 1129 probably completes the resumption of the solar tradition (section VIII), since 1130 seems to do much more.

The last spell of this section and of the whole first group in de Buck's edition begins with the statement by the All-lord, Re, which enumerates his four good deeds to man. These include the equal opportunities which he gave to men, the freedom of men to act against his will, and the turning of men's thoughts toward the beyond as a spur to make them offer to the gods. A brief statement about the creation of gods and men follows. The deceased does not become Re by this spell. After the deceased has spent millions of years between Re and Osiris, they will all sit together in one place, with Re as the supreme god. A prophecy of destruction and change precede a rubric about the powers of the perfect spirit of the deceased. The book ends as it began with the deceased who knows this spell able to "be like Re in the sky," but it is added that this "is counted as being like Osiris in the midst of the underworld." Therefore it does not matter which tradition or guide of the afterlife is followed or which goal is sought,

Osiris is as good as Re, but they will be together eventually with Re supreme.

CT 1130 (101) and 1031 (101)

A,B[a] [461]WORDS SPOKEN BY HIM-WHOSE-NAMES-ARE-SECRET, the All-lord who speaks in front of the Silenced-ones who raged when the entourage sailed. [462]Proceed in peace that I may repeat to you the two[b] good deeds which[c] my own[d] heart has done for me in the midst of the coiled one in order to silence evil.[e] I have done four good deeds in the midst of the portal of the horizon. I made the four winds [463]that every man might breathe[f] in his time. This is one of the deeds.[g] I made the great flood, that the poor man as well as the great one[h] might have power.[i] This is one of the deeds. I made every man like his fellow. [464]I did not command that they do evil. It is their hearts which disobey what I have said.[j] This is one of the deeds. I made their hearts to cease forgetting the West, in order to make divine offerings to the gods of the nomes. This is one of the deeds. It is with my[k] sweat that I created the gods. [465]Mankind is from the weeping of my eye. This N.[l] shines[m] with the result that he is seen every day as this dignitary[n] of the All-lord. It is for the One-who-is-weary-of-heart (Osiris) that I made night.[o] This N. will truly[p] sail in his bark. This N. is the lord of Ḥeḥu[q] in the voyage of the sky. [466]This N. has not shown respect for[r] a limb in him.[s] Authoritative-utterance and Magic overthrow for me[t] that One-of-evil-character, that this N. may see the horizon,[u] that he may sit in front of it,[v] that he may judge the poor together with the rich, [467]and that he may do[w] likewise to the evil ones. Life belongs to him. He is its possessor.
The scepter[x] was not taken from my hand.[y] This N. has spent millions of years between me and that One-who-is-weary-of-heart, the son of Geb.[z] We shall sit in one place.[aa] [468]Ruins will be cities and vice versa;[ab] house will desolate house.
THIS N. IS THE POSSESSOR OF FLAME WHO LIVES ON MAAT, THE LORD OF ETERNITY. REJOICE![ac] THE MYSTERIOUS SERPENTS HAVE

Section IX

NOT REBELLED AGAINST HIM. THIS N. IS HE-WHO-IS-IN-HIS-CHAPEL, POSSESSOR OF WOUNDS,^{ad} WHO DOES NOT RAGE, ^{469}WHO REPELS THE SERPENTS FOR^{ae} HIM-WHOSE-NAMES-ARE-NUMEROUS, THE ONE WHO GOES FORTH FROM HIS CHAPEL, THE LORD OF THE WINDS, WHO ANNOUNCES THE NORTH WIND, HE-WHOSE-NAMES-ARE-NUMEROUS IN THE MOUTH OF THE ENNEAD, LORD OF THE HORIZON, THE CREATOR, WHO ILLUMINES THE SKY WITH HIS OWN BEAUTY.^{af} N. IS THIS ONE.^{ag} MAKE WAY FOR THIS N.^{ah} ^{470}THAT HE MAY SEE NUN^{ai} AND AMUN. THIS N. IS A MYSTERIOUS^{aj} PERFECT SPIRIT. MAY HE PASS THE PROTECTORS.^{ak} THEY CANNOT SPEAK THROUGH FEAR OF HIM-WHOSE-NAME-IS-HIDDEN,^{al} WHO IS IN THE BODY OF THIS N. THIS N. KNOWS HIM. HE IS NOT IGNORANT OF HIM. ^{471}THIS N. IS EQUIPPED, EFFECTIVE IN OPENING PORTALS.^{am}

As for any person who knows this spell, he will be like Re in the east^{an} of the sky, like^{ao} Osiris in the midst of the underworld (dw_t). He will go down to the entourage of flame. There is no flame against him forever.^{ap} Thus it concludes very successfully.

---

^{a}Version A occurs in B3C, B4C, B1Bo, and B6C. Version B occurs in B1L and is also found in part on B3L. B1C and B9C have affinities to both versions A and B. For translations and descriptions of this spell cf. John A. Wilson, The Burden of Egypt, pp. 117-118; S. Morenz, Ägyptische Religion, pp. 58-59; and H. Kees, OLZ, 1962, col. 591.

^{b}B6C has "four," and B9C has the three plural strokes.

^{c}Or, "that I may repeat to you (twice), how good is what..."

^{d}B9C omits ds.i.

^{e}Instead of "in order to silence evil" B1L has "because I desired to silence evil."

^{f}B6C adds "like his fellow."

^{g}Literally "It is a deed thereof." B1L omits im.

^{h}Wr, or "rich."

^{i}B6C and B1L add "thereby."

^{j}B1L has "I did not command that evil be done by their hearts which disobey what I have said."

^{k}B6C has an original first person here while almost all the other first person pronouns in this mss. had been changed to N. pn.

^{l}Apparently the All-lord is still speaking and the first person pronouns are generally confused. I am referring to the deceased as this N. here as often as this can be determined by the name or pronouns of B3C.

   ^{m}B3C has r, "This N. will shine." B1L has "May this N. shine."

   ^{n}B3C has m sh.sn pn, "in this their booth" but B4C and B1Bo have m sʿh pn, and this suits the following genetive better. B9C has m shd pw, "as this inspector," or is like B1L which has "every day when I illumine the sky for the All-lord." B1C has "as this exorcisor."

   ^{o}B1C and B1L have "I made day for Healthy and night for He-who-is-weary-of-heart."

   ^{p}B1L omits mẖʿ. B6C omits r and with walking-legs determinative on mẖʿ has "This N. (will) sail having set out in his own bark."

   ^{q}B1L has "I am the lord who gives water." B6C and B9C have nhh "eternity" for hhw.

   ^{r}B6C and B9C have "I cannot respect."

   ^{s}B1C has "in him" after a subject in the first person so perhaps B3C changed the gender of this pronoun incorrectly.

   ^{t}B6C adds "the enemy of this N." B4C had iw.i hnʿ.i for iw Hw at the beginning of the sentence, an obvious error.

   ^{u}B3C omits "the Horizon."

   ^{v}B6C, B9C and B1L have "its outer chamber."

   ^{w}B3C omits ir N. tn.

   ^{x}B3C and perhaps B4C add grt, "moreover."

   ^{y}B3C has "from me."

   ^{z}B6C omits "son." B1C and B1L have "Nut." cf. Hans Goedicke, <u>The Report about the Dispute of a Man with his Ba</u>, p. 80 note 206, for a different translation of this sentence.

   ^{aa}B6C and B9C have "I/N. shall sit with him in one place." B1L has "(I) shall sit in one place."

   ^{ab}B4C has "and the cities will be mounds." B1C and B1L have "I have made ruins into cities and vice versa."

   ^{ac}B1L begins the rubric "MAAT IS LORD OF ETERNITY. REJOICE!"

   ^{ad}B1L adds s "its wounds" or perhaps "their wounds."

   ^{ae}B1L omits n.

   ^{af}B1L has "The creator, in his own form."

   ^{ag}B3C adds "In his name" and B4C has "In her name." B3L omits the particle i.

   ^{ah}B1L omits this statement.

   ^{ai}Written niw.

   ^{aj}B1L omits ʿftt.

   ^{ak}Nhẖw also occur in Amduat, II, 65. B9C has hnw "the family." B1L has msw "the children." The rest of version A in B3C is CT 1031. This begins with "^{262}THAT WHICH IS AT THE END OF THE BOOK."

Section IX

^{al}B1L has "[ME] WHOSE NAME IS HIDDEN."

^{am}B9C adds "his" and continues "[I] made [. . .] in my [. . .] that he might pass in peace."

^{an}B1L omits ḫbt.

^{ao}B1C has "which is counted (as being) like..."

^{ap}B1L has "The one who flames against him will not exist forever and ever."

The purpose of the last section was to put together the separate traditions, to arrange them according to their rank (perhaps based on earlier social distinctions) and to provide the means (spells) whereby anyone (who could afford the book) could reach the highest goal (Re). Versions A and B of the Book of Two Ways, then, are a description of the "democratization of the hereafter" as well as propaganda for the cult of Re.

CONCLUSION

The texts written on the bottoms of Middle Kingdom coffins from el Barsha, which Egyptologists call the Book of Two Ways, were "guides to the beyond" that were supposed to provide the deceased with the means of obtaining a desirable afterlife. The ancient Egyptians clearly treated it as a book with a beginning and an end as we see from the colophons, particularly that of spell 1031. They also recognized that the book had several versions since the coffins of some persons contained two or even three versions of it.[1] They may or may not have realized how different these versions were. If they did, some of them probably did not know which was really better and therefore tried to be safe by having more than one version. The copies that survive probably date fairly close together, and their sources were compiled somewhat earlier from material that was often considerably earlier.

The book actually has four versions including two that are almost entirely different (A and C), another (B) that is based on the plan of A with some substitutions and with its texts generally more like those of version C, and finally a small group (A-B) that has affinities to both A and B. Version A is represented on B3C, B4C, B12C, B13C, B6C, B4L, B1Bo, and B4Bo. Version C is represented on B5C, B1Be, B1P, and B4L. Version B occurs on B1L, B2L, B3L, and B2P. Version A-B occurs on B2Bo, B9C, and B1C. The earliest of these versions is probably version C. and this is inferred from the contents of the spells, generally because the other versions seem to start with this version and by adding to it and by changing its orientation make it much more attractive to the people who wanted such a guide. Version A came next since version B repeated the conclusion of section V from both versions A and C. The A-B version is not a distinct group whose manuscripts are closely related to one another, but, in different places, one or the other of the manuscripts is closer to one or the other versions, and so all three manuscripts seem to depend on both A and B.

Conclusion

135

The main purpose of this "guide" was to enable the deceased to attain a goal, but the goal of version C is not the same as the goal of the other versions. The introduction to version C (CT 1131) makes it clear that the goal of the deceased is to see Osiris, live beside him and rot beside him. To attain this goal, the deceased must know the names of the demons who guard the doors of the horizon and must know how to recognize them. Section II occurs only in version C and it pictures doors and names the demon keepers to be passed in order to reach a mansion which is illustrated at the end of the section (CT 1146). In passing the doors and demons, the deceased is described as a pilot of the solar bark, but the goal reached is apparently the mansion of Osiris. Sections III and IV depict the water and land ways which represent the sky and the underworld. This cosmological plan names and illustrates the demons encountered by the pilot of the solar bark in his circuitous daytime and night-time voyage and also includes the nocturnal voyage of Thoth's lunar bark on the same waterway used by the sun god during the day. On this plan the "Field of Hetep" or "Field of Offerings" of Osiris is found in the western sky. Section V describes the "ways of Rosetaw" on land and water. It names more demons and states that anyone who knows their names will see Osiris and live forever.

The goal of all the other versions is to join the sungod, Re. The introduction to versions A and B clearly emphasizes Re and the journey of his solar bark until, in CT 1034 and 1035, the description and purpose of the guide are stated and the two other major gods, Osiris and Thoth, are introduced. In CT 1035 it is said that any person who knows this spell will be a god in the suite of Thoth.

Following this introduction, versions A and B continue with the same plan of the two ways that was found in the middle of the C-version. The important difference is that two spells which were not in version C (CT 1065 and 1099) were apparently added here as part of a revision in favor of Re over Osiris. While the other spells along the land way describe the voyage of Re in his bark at night and look forward to his rising in the morning, these two spells describe both the day and night voyage and stress the supremacy of Re over all.

Section V is for the most part the same as it was in

version C, but the long conclusion in C was shortened in A possibly because this original conclusion had been so completely Osirian. In version B the endings of section V from both A and C were repeated. The reasoning behind the whole B-version and probably A-B seems to be an uncertainty about which of the two sources was better. The scribes who compiled these later versions used the plan of version A probably because it was longer and apparently more complete, and they used the texts of C in those sections that were paralleled perhaps because they knew that these were earlier. Whether or not the scribes of these later versions knew what they were doing is debatable, but they did apparently intend to have the same ultimate goal as version A, and one obvious change from Osiris to Re was made at the end of spell 1085.

Section VI in the long versions presents a tradition about the beyond that makes the moon god, Thoth, and his abode in the sky the goal of the deceased. The long spell 1099 of section VII is a full description of the voyage of the deceased on the solar bark, and is thus another tradition about the afterlife, this time involving Re. CT 1065 in section IV was probably the beginning of this spell which was misplaced in the Book of Two Ways since both 1065 and 1099 describe the complete solar voyage and both survive together as a single chapter in the Book of the Dead. In section VIII seven doors and doorkeepers must be known by the deceased so that he can lead the solar bark of the elder Horus past them.

The conclusion of the whole book in section IX ties together these previous traditions and relates them to one another at the same time. It quotes from previous sections and illustrates the gods in the shrines on their barks which were described or pictured earlier. First the lunar tradition is resumed and theoretically the deceased who knows the spells up to this point will be able to join Thoth as a star in the sky. If he knows the next few spells which refer to the mansion, bark and sealed place of Osiris, he will be more glorious than Osiris. Finally if he knows all the spells, he will be with Re, the great creator god who made all men equal in opportunity.[2]

Having these traditions related to one another in terms of knowledge of the spells for reaching one, then another, goal is a convenient way to demonstrate that the person who reaches

Conclusion

Re has reached the highest goal. This is the way we would expect a priest of Re to try to show that his religion had more to offer than the other popular religions of his time. By taking over an important document of the Osiris religion and turning this into a part of a treatise which gives all the tenets of the Re religion and holds forth a more desirable goal in the afterlife, the priest who composed this version was probably trying to convert people. However, the priest was also convinced that no matter which religion people believed in they would eventually share in the same afterlife that he described and Re would be the supreme god.

Another relationship between these goals that was probably intentional on the part of the priest who composed version A, is found in his breaking down earlier social distinctions which would not have permitted a common man to reach this highest goal. There is no way to tell when if ever such class distinctions with regard to the beyond would have been thought to have existed or would have been overcome, but it does seem that they are broken down in this document. If being a star in the sky with Thoth were the goal of a commoner and living in the Field of Osiris were the goal of a "great man," then certainly everyone would be eager to be able to attain the goal of a king which all knew was to join Re on the sun bark.

The fact that all of the versions of the <u>Book of Two Ways</u> come from a cemetery of Hermopolis may show us that priests of different religions were competing with one another within this one city. Either that or the local priests of Thoth were very adaptable to the cults that swept the nation. Such speculation can perhaps be put on a firmer footing when more work has been done with the rest of the <u>Coffin Texts</u>. In any case the speculation based on the <u>Pyramid Texts</u> that there was an Osirinization of original solar texts[3] is not borne out here perhaps because the trend had reversed itself.

Some of the interesting observations that have been made about the <u>Book of Two Ways</u> in the past do not apply to this guidebook at all. This is because texts which do not belong to the book were often included on the bottoms of coffins in available space at the end of a register or within an enclosure, and the Egyptologists who looked at individual copies did not realize that some of the texts were really additional material.

While some coffins had too many spells, most had too few. Since de Buck had eighteen coffins to work with, he was able to bring the book back very close to its original form. He realized that the book had two distinct versions and he edited them separately. For purposes of comparison, I have placed these two versions side by side, and I have made further changes from the order of the texts in de Buck's edition when such changes seemed warranted. The arrangement of these texts was obviously very important to the scribes since even very incomplete manuscripts with only parts of spells or parts of sections still had these parts in their proper order.

The arrangement of all the religious texts on the Middle Kingdom coffins is now being studied particularly with regard to other apparent and real contradictions in them. Another group of texts in Coffin Texts that have a connection with the Book of Two Ways is concerned with the Field of Hetep,[4] and this group was probably one of the first included on these same coffins and presents this field as being more attractive than it appears in the Book of Two Ways.

Grapow early pointed out that a great part of the Book of Two Ways had been introduced into the Book of the Dead.[5] One might reasonably expect that the Book of the Dead along with Amduat and the Book of Gates should be included in a study of the work's Nachleben rather than its Vorleben, but the results of the present study seem to show that what material Book of Two Ways and Book of the Dead share would have preexisted the Book of Two Ways. It can be argued from the separation of BD 130 into two parts (CT 1065 and 1099) that the related chapter in the Book of the Dead probably did not come from the Book of Two Ways, but that the book had a source in common whose spells were closer in form to their appearance in the Book of the Dead. This can also be argued from two similar breaks in continuity at the beginning of section V. We have a different argument from section I where the Book of the Dead chapter was fuller yet lacking in anything that would restrict it to introducing the Book of Two Ways. Finally the "Field of Offerings" as presented in CT 1047-1052 is not the source of BD 110, but the source of both seems to be represented in CT 464-468.

Notes to Conclusion

[1] The inner coffin of Sepi, B2P, has the B-version while his outer coffin, B1P, has version C. The outer coffin of Sen, B4L, begins with the plan of the water and land ways according to version C and concludes with the plan according to version A, while his inner coffin, B3L, has the whole B-version.

[2] There is certainly no need to explain the Book of Two Ways as a plan of a temple with three sanctuaries at the back, as has recently been suggested by Barguet (Rd'É 21 [1969] 7-17) since there would be no reason to have the approach to a temple divided by a river of flame, there is really no equality in the shrines at the end, and that a temple would be filled with demons is inexplicable.

[3] James H. Breasted, Development of Religion and Thought in Ancient Egypt. (New York, [originally 1912], 1959), pp. 142-164.

[4] Cf. L. H. Lesko, "The Field of Ḥetep in Egyptian Coffin Texts," JARCE (forthcoming).

[5] Hermann Grapow, "Zweiwegebuch und Totenbuch," ZÄS 46 (1909) 77.

INDEX OF CT SPELLS

CT	page	CT	page	CT	page
513	90	1062	68	1097	99
577	91	1063	67	1098	100
1029	11	1064	66,67	1099	102
1030	13	1065	65	1100	109
1031	130	1066	64	1101	110
1032	15	1067	64	1102	111
1033	16	1068	61	1103	112
1034	20	1069	63,62	1104	113
1035	20	1070	78	1105	113
1036	40	1071	77	1106	114
1037	42	1072	80	1107	114
1038	43	1073	81	1108	115
1039	44	1074	82	1109	115
1040	44	1075	82	1110	116
1041	45	1076	83	1111	117
1042	47	1077	83	1112	117
1043	50	1078	84	1113	118
1044	49	1079	84	1114	119
1045	50	1080	86	1115	120
1046	51	1081	86	1116	120
1047	52	1082	88	1117	122
1048	52	1083	87	1118	123
1049	54	1084	92,88	1119	123
1050	55	1085	88	1120	124
1051	55	1086	85	1121	125
1052	77,56	1087	86	1122	125
1053	57	1088	93	1123	125
1054	59	1089	94	1124	126
1055	75	1090	97	1125	126
1056	75	1091	98	1126	127
1057	73	1092	98	1127	127
1058	73	1093	93	1128	128
1059	72	1094	96	1129	128
1060	71	1095	98	1130	130
1061	69	1096	99	1131	23

CT	page	CT	page
1132	25	1171	66
1133	26	1172	69
1134	27	1173	68
1135	28	1174	68, 67
1136	29	1175	70
1137	30	1176	63, 65
1138	31	1177	64
1139	31	1178	63
1140	32	1179	62
1141	33	1180	77
1142	34	1181	78
1143	34	1182	80
1144	35	1183	81
1145	36	1184	82
1146	38	1185	84
1147	40		
1148	42		
1149	46		
1150	45		
1151	47		
1152	46		
1153	58		
1154	49		
1155	50		
1156	50		
1157	58		
1158	51		
1159	53		
1160	54		
1161	53		
1162	55		
1163	56		
1164	55		
1165	58		
1166	59		
1167	75		
1168	73		
1169	71		
1170	68		

BOOK OF THE DEAD PARALLELS

Chapter	page
4	82
117	84, 85
118	45
119	88
130	65, 102
133	11
135	117
136	13, 16, 20, 65
144	44, 45, 46, 47, 49, 52, 53, 62, 63, 64, 68, 69, 70, 71, 72, 73, 75, 77, 78, 109
147	77, 78, 81, 82, 84, 85, 88, 111, 112
179	90, 91

INDEX OF SELECTED VOCABULARY

3y (for 3ry?) oppressor 292 b

3bḥw ⸢abeḥu-plants⸣ 424 b

3bḫ (for bḫḫ?) burn 263 a

3bs (for 3sb) fierce 499 h

3ry oppressor 501 k

3rt dung 327 a, 516 a

3ḥi miserable 287 d

3ḫw ⸢scum⸣ 413 b

3sb fierce 288 c, 499 h

3srt (?) 428 b

3sti trembler 292 d

3s̆bw (for 3sbw ?) Fierce-one 296 d

3gb flood 413 b, 421 b, 463 c

3tw burn 371 a, b

3tw (3dw) aggressor 309 a, 509 k, 310 a, 503 g, 516 e, 510 e, 424 a, 423 a, 483 n, 489 j, 494 a

3tn (?) 477 f

3di Furious-one 292 d

3dmw ⸢glow⸣ 297 d

i33w (i33t) ⸢Rod⸣ 369 b, 333 a

i3s bald 450 d

i3dw pestilence 412 c

iʿrw (for iʿrt ?) abode 481 c

iw (in ḫr-iw) Transgressor 370 l

iw cry out 456 e

iwtiw corruption 365 f

ibib contentment 411 b

ibt to snare, a trap 254 b, 483 g

ip3 to fly 472 i

imy-ʿ ⸢fetters⸣ 485 l, 487 e

imy-wr westerner 276 b

ynisf (?) 473 e

inn delay 311 c

innwt traps 473 m

intt fetters 377 a

irw-ḥ3dw trap-maker 493 a

irtt (for itt ?) 310 a

iḥ pain 521 c, 351 a

iḥm lingering 350 d

iḥ3wy (for ʿḥ3) warriors 490 d

iḥy sistrum-player 492 d, 447 a

iḫwtit (?) 304 j, 507 a

ikw (?) 488 m

iknty (?) 420 a

itʿ ⸢seize⸣ 453 g

itnw ⸢radiant⸣ 256 a

itt fly up 310 a

id ⸢dampen⸣ 275 a

idnt ⸢substitution⸣ 270 a

ꜥꜣp   reproach   482 g

ꜣtỉw   ꜥAatiu   306 d, 508 e

ꜣtỉm   (?)   288 g

ꜣtt   (?)   288 d, 306 d, 508 e

ꜥwꜥw (for ỉwꜥ)   heir   323 b

ꜥwnt   plunderer   322 b

ꜥbꜣt   ⌜stroke⌝   283 b

ꜥbbwt   spear   457 n

ꜥff   a fly   472 i

ꜥfnwt   Wrapped-up   478 j

ꜥftt   mysterious   278 c, 304 e, 518 a, 447 e, 468 e, 470 b

ꜥmꜣwt   throwstick   342 b, 425 b

ꜥmꜥ   male   492 c, 450 d

ꜥmꜥt   female   450 d

ꜥnnty (ꜥnt)   claw, nail   434 b, 472 h, 485 l

ꜥnṯ (for ꜥnt?)   489 h

ꜥrḳ   bind   258 b

ꜥtỉꜣḥwt   (?)   499 e

wꜥꜣw   curse, Blasphemer   288 f, 291 b, 499 j

wꜥb(y)t   tomb   317 a

wꜥbb   be clean, purify   357 d, 487 c

wbs   ⌜water-flood⌝   388 c

wbs   ⌜rise⌝   395 a, 410 c

wbd (wbḏ)   burn   263 a

wnn   hasten   510 j

wnšw   ⌜arrows⌝   494 f

wsrnn   Usernen   476 b

wsṯ   decay   VI 97 i

wš   desolation   468 b

wḏbw (with rd)   reversion-offerings   297 e

bꜣwt (?)   Dendera   481 f

bꜣbꜣ   socket, hole   472 f, 480 g, 495 a

bꜣs (?)   jar   447 a

bꜣḳ   dazzle   373 a, b

bꜣd (?)   450 d

bỉꜣw   Biau   401 c

bꜥt (for wꜥbt?)   512 f

bbt   bebet-herb   424 c

bnwt   ⌜baboons⌝   366 h

bnt   ⌜sweets⌝   305 a

bḥ (or bḫ for bḥḥ)   drive off   263 a

bsy   Blaser   335 d

bsn   harm   351 d

bḳsw   vertebrae   254 a

btn (btnn)   defiant   472 b, 473 d

btḳtḳ   Escaper   494 i

btkw   squalor   476 d

bṯ   abandon   453 a

bṯṯ   run   510 e

pꜣḥ   scratch   491 d

pgpỉ (?)   499 i

pt   canopy   446 b

fnṯw   worms, snakes   437 f, 480 g

Indexes   145

fdt sweat 464 g

mꜣstỉw (mꜣsw) squatters 342 a, 520 a, 351 b, 354 b

my ꜥEqualizerꜣ 292 b

mꜥꜣt throwstick 342 b

mwy to water 375 a

mmt ꜥmemet-plantꜣ 424 d

mswr drinking-place 446 b

mdw staff 407 b, 394 b

mdsw sharp-ones 355 e, 502 c, VI 193 e

mḏtn boat (for mꜥnḏt ?) 488 f

nꜣw breezes 338 b

nỉꜣ rejected 369 b

nỉw Nun 470 a

nwrw Trembler 495 j

nwḏ suffer 385 c, 420 b

nbtt basket 301 f

nfꜣ evil 332 b, 516 g

nfw sailors 487 g

nmw Nemu 508 h, 488 n

nmmm quiver 255 a

nhꜣ protector 470 c

nhd furious 297 c, 503 i

nḥꜣ contrary 208 a, 370 d, 479 b

nḥbty necky 370 c, 369 b, 482 h

nḥt prayer 491 e

nḥꜣ winding, recurved 458 m, 259 b

nḥꜣw ꜥThose who are twistedꜣ 338 b

nḥn young 312 a, 511 c

nḥnḥ Nekhenekh 480 i

nḫḫ Old-one 486 e, 488 k, 490 j

nsps (?) 489 a

nsrw Flaming-one 366 f

nsḥwḥ (?) 475 d

nss fire 262 i, 297 c, 503 i

nt water 368 b

nṯ tongue 422 b

ndp experience 482 c

r-ỉwꜣ ꜥcabinꜣ 278 b

rw straw 299 b, 300 b

rwf (rwḏ) ꜥsuperintendentꜣ 403 d

rḥḥ celebrated 383 a

rḳḳt enmity 473 d

rd growing-plant, grow 478 b, 485 h

hꜣ drip down 368 b

hꜣb (hb) write 473 n

hỉ low 443 a

hỉw confusion 501 e, 292 c, 421 a, 376 a

hb plough through 498 i

hn box 483 c

hny joy 257 b

hnw family 470 c

hh blast 441 c, 412 a, 435 a, 489 h

ḥꜣ bewail 299 b

ḫȝy   protector   492 c

ḫȝf (for ḫfȝ ?)   338 a

ḫȝmt   excrement   423 b

ḫȝt   blot out, dispel   441 a, c, 393 c, 408 b, 426 c, 369 d, 373 b

ḫȝt   prow-rope   416 a

ḫȝd   to trap   493 b

ḫʿȝ   children   392 c

ḫʿw   ⌈shell⌉   460 e

ḫʿs   (?)   497 h

ḫw   sticks   520 b, 342 b

ḫwȝ   rot   473 h

ḫwt   rain   370 f

ḫbd-r   Opener-of-mouth   485 l, m, 486 d

ḫn   to command   489 g

ḫnwt   a command   489 e

ḫnt   waters   476 i

ḫrntf   Ḥernetjef   435 c

ḫrr   above   502 d

ḫry-š   garden   490 c

ḫḫw   chaos-gods   347 e

ḫtf   (?)   489 g

ḫts   (?)   483 c

ḫdk   cut off   472 f

ḫdn   ⌈Rager⌉   486 g

ḫȝbȝs   starry host   258 a

ḫȝsf   ⌈morbid⌉   337 c

ḫbt(iw)   place of execution, Executioners   317 d, 513 f

ḫmwt   exclude   312 a

ḫm   destroyer   487 c

ḫnfȝ   ⌈pretentious⌉   332 b

ḫnm   take care of, attendant   505 b, 505 f

ḫnmt   ⌈fragrant-food⌉   299 c, 301 c, g

ḫrḫr   destroy   491 d

ḫḫt   Khekhet   511 c

ḫtỉ   to carve   482 b

ḫtỉ   to retreat   370 b

ḫtyw   Fiery-ones   486 f

ḫtm   to seal   472 f

ẖȝsw   ⌈corpse⌉   323 b, 513 b, 514 b

ẖȝty   storm   440 e

ẖnnw   uproar   452 d, 493 k

ẖrw   underlings   487 f,   m ẖrw downward 305 d

ẖrt-ʿ   writing materials   365 e

sȝȝt   guardian   477 c

sȝỉt   ⌈chest⌉   452 e

sȝyš (for sȝy ?)   499 b

sȝmt   lock   472 f

sȝḫ   cut off   485 l, 487 h

sȝš (sȝḫ)   open   451 e

sỉw   announcer   451 c

sỉn   rub   450 d

sỉrtỉw (for srt ?)   ⌈sheep⌉   499 g

sʿbȝ   prepare   277 c

Indexes

s'fn cover 472 h
swtiw ⌈reed-dwellers⌉ 265 b
swtt ⌈sutet-bird⌉ 495 e
swꜣš applaud 480 i
sbb send, conduct 328 a, 507 g, 515 f
sbg the planet Mercury 261 a
spꜣ centipede 453 h
spꜣ Sepa 481 k
sfꜣ mild 516 g
sfꜣ to hate 293 c, 501 c
sm to aid 481 p
smꜣw locks 256 a
smḥ boat 480 h
smtw Investigator 296 i
snf Bloody-one 494 e
snḥ bind 474 j, 480 k
snšw double-doors 325 a, 324 d
sntw rebellious 401 a
srtiw ⌈knives⌉ 416 c
shiw Confuser 292 c
sḥr make distant 459 b
sḥw breadth 490 e
sḥd upside-down 436 h
sḥwt (for ḥswt Miserable-ones ?) 488 f
ssn breathe 463 a
ssḏꜣt ⌈what is sealed⌉ 448 a
sšm (?) butcher 417 a
sšnt ⌈lotus-prowed boat⌉ 259 a
sšd headband 258 b

sk sweep 361 a
skm grey-haired one 492 d
stwt resemble 473 i
stwt ⌈assemblage⌉ 452 b
stnm opposite direction 519 e, 340 a
sdb ⌈explain⌉ 328 c, 515 g

šꜣp Leaper 288 b
šꜣmt heat 390 b
šꜣsw (for ḥꜣsw ?) 320 b, 512 h
šy Shu 507 a, 498 d
šb Mixer 502 e
šft majestic 332 b
šnft (?) 450 d
šnpw ⌈break⌉ 487 e
šspt ⌈šspt-cloth⌉ 517 e, 333 a
šsrw arrow 494 k
št adorn 503 a, 295 d

ḳꜣs bind 388 a, 316 c, 512 b
ḳmꜣ mourn 286 c, 498 h
ḳn ⌈yellowness⌉ 378 c
ḳꜣt cow 347 k
kiw obeisance 290 b
kns Kenes 514 d
ksy Bowed-down one 482 f

gnn ⌈rough⌉ 421 b
gḥ be weary 342 a, 520 a

tȝšbw (for tšb ?)   520 i

tp-tr   beginning of the season
    496 b

tpyt   sheer   406 a

tfȝ   (for ȝtf ? crown)   475 f

tmȝtiw   judges   391 b

tkk   attacker   482 e

ṯȝ   pellet   472 f

ṯȝ   fledgling   297 b

ṯbhȝ   (Seth)   456 e

ṯnw   numbering   313 d

ṯnnwt   ⌜Tjennut-gods⌝   476 c

ṯrp   goose   484 g

dpw   steering-oar   258 b

dḫw   lowness   346 b, 520 l

dsw   ⌜Those-of-the-knives⌝
    305 c,   VI 193 e

dsrw   (for ḏsrw ?)   holy place
    313 d

ḏȝf   Heated-one   497 i

ḏȝdwt   ⌜cobra-goddess⌝   347 i

ḏwm   (mnmn ?)   travel   477 a

ḏbȝt   sarcophagus   455 a

ḏbw   (for wḏbw ?)   298 a, 504 d

ḏdft   worms   489 g

www.ingramcontent.com/pod-product-compliance
Lightning Source LLC
Chambersburg PA
CBHW021711230426
43668CB00008B/800